AF622853

Bilingual
Guide
to Japan

UKIYO-E

TANABE Masako

SHOGAKUKAN

Bilingual Guide to Japan

UKIYO-E

TANABE Masako

Book and Cover design ©Kindaichi Design

Published by
SHOGAKUKAN
2-3-1 Hitotsubashi Chiyoda-ku,
Tokyo 101-8001 JAPAN
https://www.shogakukan.co.jp/
https://japanesebooks.jp/en/

All rights reserved.
No part of this publication may be reproduced in any form or by any means, graphic, electronic or mechanical, including photocopying and recording by an information storage and retrieval system, without written permission from the publisher.

UKIYO-E BILINGUAL GUIDE by
TANABE Masako
©2024 Masako Tanabe / SHOGAKUKAN
Printed in Japan
ISBN 978-4-09-389171-4

浮世絵バイリンガルガイド

田辺昌子 著

小学館

English Renderings of UKIYO-E

This English and Japanese bilingual book introduces the basic knowledge and representative types of ukiyo-e.
All Japanese terms are rendered in italicized Roman characters.
The only diacritical mark used is the hyphen.

Since the conventions for rendering these terms into English differ depending on the facility, terms used elsewhere may not be consistent with those used in this book. Given that even Japanese names and pronunciations may differ depending on the sect or region, they cannot be generalized. Standard names are used in this book and are rendered so that they can be easily read by individuals who are not native speakers of Japanese.

All ukiyo-e prints in this book are indicated as *oban nishiki-e*, meaning a *nishiki-e* color woodblock print, in ink and color on the *oban* format. Although the size and quality of ukiyo-e paper varied depending on where it was produced, the *oban* format is considered to have a standard size of approximately 38 cm × 25 cm, based on one half of a full-size sheet of paper from Iyo Province (present-day Ehime prefecture), which was commonly used after 1772.

本書の英文表記について

この本は、代表的な浮世絵について紹介しています。日本語が母語ではない人のために、英語で訳してあります。
日本語はローマ字読みにし、斜体のアルファベットで表記しています。発音しにくい長い単語はハイフン(–)を使用しています。

※これら外国語表記は、施設（公共施設、地方自治体等）ごとに異なるルールで表記されているため、本書と一致しない場合があります。地方によって日本語でも呼び方が異なることがあり、一般化はできません。本書では標準的な呼称を掲載し、外国語を母語とする読者ができるだけ平易に発音できる表記としました。
※本書の浮世絵の判型は、大半が「大判錦絵」です。浮世絵の紙は、産地によって大きさや質が異なりますが、安永期（1772–81）以降に多く使用された伊予産の大奉書全紙判の半切が大判で、約38cm×25cmが標準的です。

Table of Contents 目次

Introduction

What Is Ukiyo-e?

Ukiyo-e emerged during the Edo period (1603-1867) in Japan's new capital of Edo (present-day Tokyo), developing principally among townspeople as a style of *fuzokuga* (genre painting). Ukiyo-e can be classified into two types: *nikuhitsuga* (brush paintings) and *hanga* (prints). Brush paintings, mainly produced on commision by ukiyo-e artists, were created on *kakejiku* (hanging scrolls) or *byobu* (screens) and almost exclusively enjoyed by wealthier patrons. Ukiyo-e prints, however, owing to three particular merits, heralded the rise of a unique culture bringing art to those from all walks of life.

Firstly, prints could be mass-produced. This allowed for easy, widespread distribution and a far greater audience for the artworks. Secondly, they were inexpensive—equivalent, it is said, to the cost of a bowl of soba noodles. Ukiyo-e prints were intended not for the wealthy and wellborn, but for the common people. Of course, to allow for this a thin margin of profit, reliant on the prints' mass appeal, was vital to balancing costs, such as the artist's fees, materials like woodblocks, paper,

はじめに

●浮世絵とは

江戸時代（1603-1867）、浮世絵は日本の新しい首都となった江戸の地（現在の東京）に生まれ、主に町人たちの間で発達した風俗画の様式です。浮世絵には、筆で描く肉筆画と、版画がありますが、浮世絵師への注文制作が中心の肉筆画は、掛軸や屏風の形式に表装され、比較的裕福な人々が楽しむものでした。一方で版画は、次の3つのメリットから、庶民に至るまで絵を楽しむことができるという世界にも稀な文化を形成することになります。

1つ目は、版画だけに量産できるという点です。その普及性の高さから、絵が大衆の手に渡るようになりました。2つ目は、価格が安いということです。浮世絵版画は、身分

and pigments, and the artisans' wages. Thirdly, prints could be planned and produced at rapid speeds, owing to an efficient and rational division of labor facilitated by *hanmoto* (publishers): artists created the designs, *horishi* (carvers) crafted the blocks, and *surishi* (printers) produced the impressions. As a result, popular interests and trends could be swiftly represented as images and shared with the world in a timely manner. Ukiyo-e prints gave visual expression to the currents of the time, be it fashion, performances of kabuki theater with popular actors, or well-known leisure quarters. The pages that follow focus on works known as *nishiki-e* (lit. brocade prints), which utilized the advanced technique of multicolor woodblock printing, and introduce their remarkable and enduring charm.

ある裕福な層ではなく、常に庶民を享受者のターゲットにしていました。その値段は、かけ蕎麦1杯程度であったといわれています。もちろん、そのためには、絵師の画料ばかりでなく、版木、紙、絵の具といった材料費、職人たちの手間賃、そして大衆に喜ばれ大量に売れるという薄利多売の採算が成立することが条件となります。そして3つ目は、版元のプロデュースにより企画され、絵師が版下絵を描き、彫師が版を製作して、摺師が摺るという、合理的な分業によって速く生産できたという点です。これによって大衆が関心を持つ流行の事象を絵に取り入れ、素早くこの商品を世に送ることができたのです。ファッション、上演中の歌舞伎や人気役者、人気の行楽地と、いち早く流行をビジュアルで伝えたのは浮世絵版画でした。この本では、特に高度な多色摺木版画技法を用いた「錦絵」と呼ばれる作品を中心に、その魅力を紹介します。

Edo Society in Bloom and the Birth of Ukiyo-e

The term *ukiyo* (lit. floating world) refers to the present or "now." Its artworks invite us to relive the vibrant heyday of Edo. Before the Edo period, Kyoto was the capital of Japan, and Edo, distant from the bustling center, was perceived as a forlorn place with few notable sites. Under the Tokugawa shogunate, however, the city was transformed. Successive shoguns constructed roads and waterways around their residence, Edo Castle, provided entertainment in the form of the Yoshiwara pleasure quarters (p. 104) and theaters, and planted cherry trees across Ueno, Gotenyama, and the banks of the Sumida River for the enjoyment of the people, bringing the city to life.

Their efforts had a further aim: that of fostering attachment to the city among its many new arrivals. By the year 1680, during the 8th year of the Empo era, with memories of the tumultuous conflicts of the 16th century diminishing and the enduring peace fostering a sense of calm and security, the earliest documented instances of the terms "ukiyo-e" and "ukiyo-e artist" were recorded. Over the next 200 years, the readily accessible

●江戸社会の繁栄と浮世絵の誕生

「浮世」は、「今」を意味する言葉でもあります。浮世絵の鑑賞を通して、我々もまた活気ある江戸という都市（現在の東京）を追体験することができるでしょう。首都が京都にあった江戸時代より前、この地には知られる名所もほとんどなく、都から離れた寂しい場所というイメージがありました。それが徳川将軍家の居城である江戸城を中心に、道路・水路といったインフラが整備され、さらに幕府は吉原遊廓（p.104）、芝居小屋の営業を公認、また町人が花を楽しめるよう上野や御殿山、隅田川の堤などに桜を植えるなど、娯楽も用意して、活気ある都市に変貌させたのです。

それは新しく流入してきた人々が、江戸という都市に愛着を持てるようにするための作業でもありました。16世紀末まで続いた戦乱の世の記憶も薄れ、太平の世が続く安堵感が江戸を満たしていたであろう時期の延宝8年（1680）には、初めて「浮世絵」

portrayals of everyday existence celebrated in ukiyo-e would remain a familiar presence in the lives of ordinary individuals young and old.

From Ordinary to Extraordinary: Ukiyo-e in the West

Ukiyo-e prints, mass-produced over centuries, were brought overseas with the advent of modernity in Japan. Ukiyo-e's illustrations of the capital's latest trends drastically reduced interest in outdated prints, to such an extent that old *nishiki-e* works from the Edo period were at times boiled down and recycled for paper. Even the introduction of the modern concept of "fine art" failed to bring about an aesthetic reappraisal of ukiyo-e as "art" in Japan. Instead, ukiyo-e's most enthusiastic collectors were Westerners arriving in the Meiji period (1868-1912), whose recognition of their artistic beauty ensured their preservation for posterity.

「浮世絵師」という言葉が確認されます。以降200年余、浮世絵は庶民生活の中で、子どもから大人まで気軽に買えて楽しめる絵として常に身近にあったのでした。

●西洋人に見出された浮世絵の美

長きにわたり大量に出版された浮世絵版画ですが、近代には多くが海外に渡りました。江戸の人々にとっては今の流行を描くのが浮世絵であったのですから、流行遅れのものを買おうという日本人などおらず、古い江戸時代の錦絵は、溶かして再生紙に回されることもありました。近代日本に「美術」という概念がもたらされても、浮世絵が美術品にあたるとは、当時の日本では誰も気がつくことはなかったのです。大量に廃棄されようとしていた浮世絵版画の美に気づき、その収集に意欲を燃やしたのは、明治時代（1868-1912）に来日した西洋人たちでした。

Global Admiration for Ukiyo-e Prints

In the 1880s, as ukiyo-e merchants became firmly established, more and more ukiyo-e prints began being exported overseas at affordable prices. Ukiyo-e was introduced to many Westerners for the first time, bringing a fresh wave of fascination and enthusiasm. Artists sought new artistic expression in ukiyo-e's novel aesthetics, with significant impact on their methods of visual representation. This trend, lasting from the late 19th to the early 20th century, is known as Japonisme. Its influence was extensive, encompassing countries across Europe—particularly France—North America, and even Russia.

Today, ukiyo-e prints are cherished worldwide, serving as invaluable representations of Japan's artistic heritage.

●外国人に愛された浮世絵

明治10年代には、浮世絵商という商売も確立され、一層膨大な浮世絵版画が安価に海外に渡ることになります。西洋の人々は、初めて出会う浮世絵に新鮮な驚きを感じて熱狂し、画家たちは浮世絵に新しい表現への手がかりを求めました。結果として彼らの視覚表現にも大きな変化が起こります。この19世紀後半から20世紀初めにかけての動向は、ジャポニスムと呼ばれています。その影響は、フランスを中心にヨーロッパ全域、また北米やロシアに至るまで、多くの国を巻き込んだ広い範囲に及ぶものでした。

今や浮世絵は世界中に所在し、日本を代表する美術品として知られています。

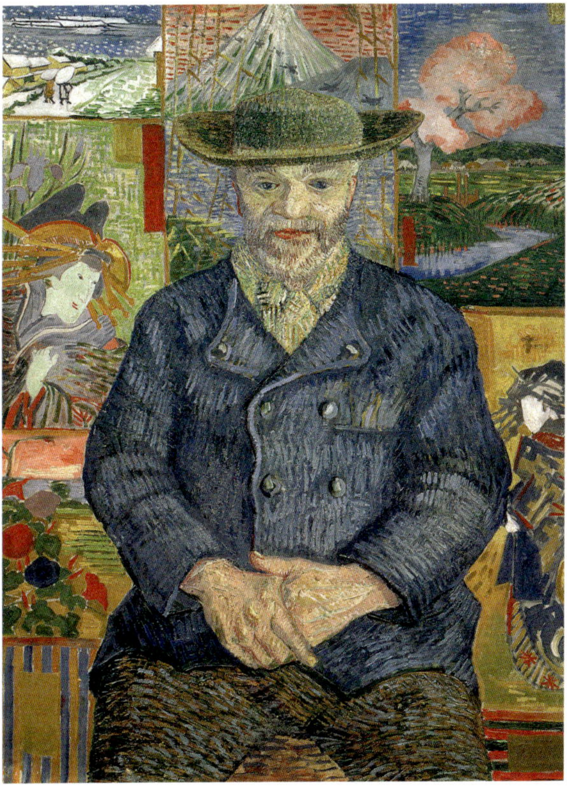

Vincent van Gogh, *Portrait of Père Tanguy,*
ca. 1887, oil on canvas. Musée Rodin.

Ukiyo-e works fill the background of Van Gogh's portrait of the beloved paint dealer Julien-François Tanguy, affectionately known as "Père Tanguy." Van Gogh was deeply influenced by Japan and was known to collect ukiyo-e prints.

フィンセント・ファン・ゴッホ「タンギー爺さん」
油彩、カンヴァス　1887年頃　ロダン美術館所蔵
慕っていた画材屋「タンギー爺さん」の肖像の背景に、ゴッホは浮世絵を描き込みました。ゴッホは日本に傾倒し、浮世絵を集めていたことが知られています。

Bridgeman Images / DNPartcom

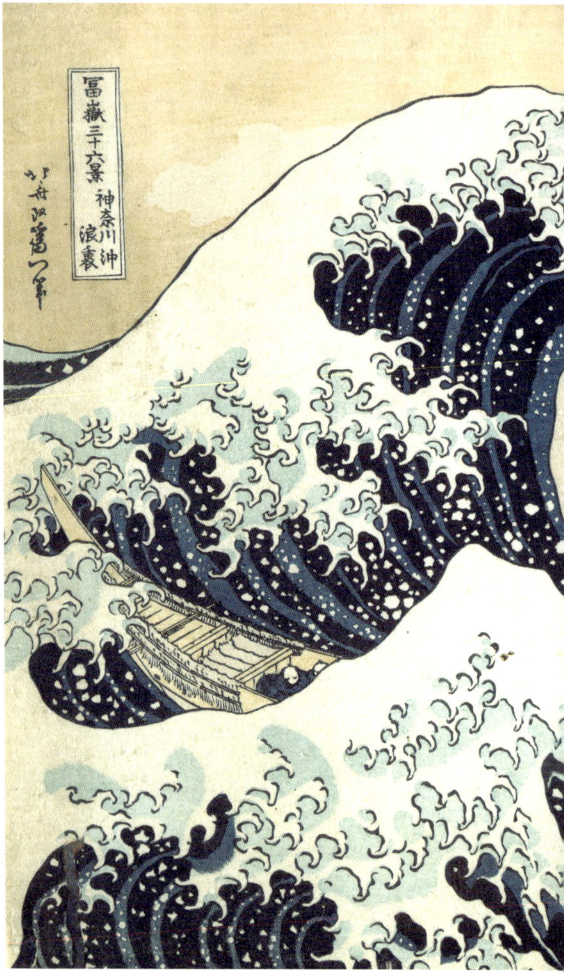

Katsushika Hokusai, *Under the Wave off Kanagawa*, from the series *Thirty-six Views of Mount Fuji*,
ca. 1831-33, *oban nishiki-e*. The Metropolitan Museum of Art.

Hokusai's *The Great Wave* is one of the most famous works of ukiyo-e, inspiring numerous Western artists. The crashing seas conjured up in the momentous final movement of Debussy's orchestral work *La Mer* found their visual counterpart in Hokusai's masterful depiction of a cresting wave.

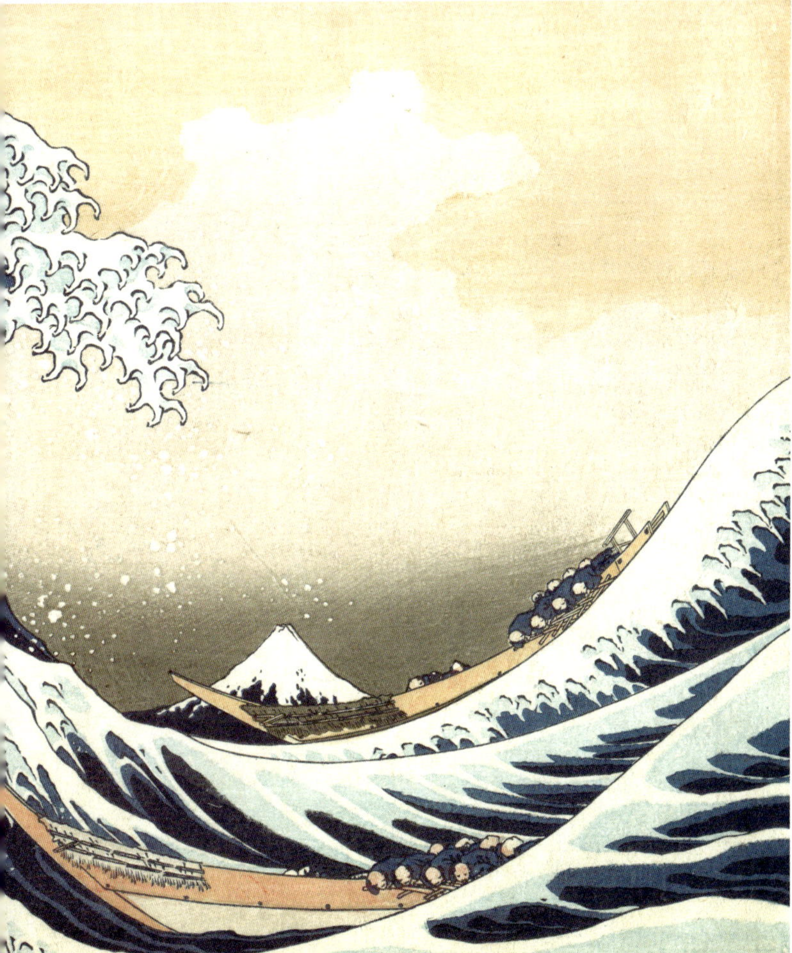

葛飾北斎「冨嶽三十六景　神奈川沖浪裏」

大判錦絵　天保2-4年（1831-33）頃　メトロポリタン美術館所蔵

この北斎の作品は、浮世絵の中でも世界で最も有名で、多くの西洋の芸術家にインスピレーションを与えました。ドビュッシーの管弦楽曲「海（La Mer）」の最終部分で演奏される激しい荒波のイメージが、北斎の描く波に重ねられたようです。

Cover of French composer Claude Debussy's *La Mer*,
published in 1905 by A. Durand & Fils.
Courtesy of Sibley Music Library, Eastman School of Music.

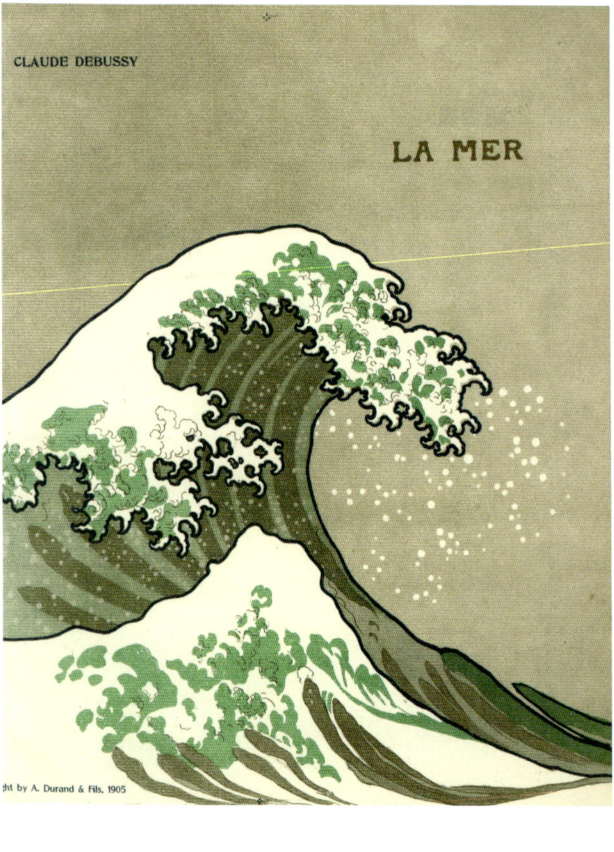

クロード・ドビュッシー 管弦楽曲
「海（La Mer）」
楽譜表紙　1905年
イーストマン音楽学校 シブリー音楽図書館提供

Chapter 1

Fundamentals of Ukiyo-e

第一章

浮世絵の基礎知識

What Are *Nishiki-e*?

The first ukiyo-e prints were simple black-and-white works made with *sumi* ink, known as *sumizuri-e*. For over sixty years, artists hand-painted color onto *sumizuri-e* prints whenever required. It wasn't until the mid-18th century that a revolutionary change occurred with the introduction of color printing using multiple woodblocks. This advanced technique was perfected around 1765 and heralded the multicolor *nishiki-e* print. First, the artist's original design was pasted face down onto a woodblock. Next, the lines were meticulously carved out, producing the *omohan*, or key block, which was used to determine color separations by making several test prints—a process known as *kyogozuri*. Typically, a separate block was carved for each color. When finished, the woodblocks were handed to the printer. Both the key block and the color blocks would have *kento* (registration marks) carved into them. The printer would use these to align the paper, layering the colors accordingly to create the beautiful *nishiki-e* prints we know today.

錦絵とは

浮世絵発祥の当初は、墨だけを用いた素朴な版画（墨摺絵）でした。色彩が求められても、墨摺絵に筆で彩色する時代が60年余続きましたので、18世紀半ば、版による彩色が始まったのは革命的なことといえます。特に高度な多色摺木版画技法、すなわち「錦絵」が完成されたのは明和2年（1765）頃のことです。まず絵師によって描かれた版下絵は、彫師が裏返しに板木に貼って、その線が忠実に彫り出されます（主版）。次に主版で摺った何枚かの墨摺（校合摺）で色分けをし、基本的に一色一版の色版が彫り出され、摺師に渡されます。主版と色版にはそれぞれ見当と呼ばれるマークが彫られており、摺師がそれに紙を合わせて摺り重ねることで、美しい錦絵が完成するのです。

勝川春山「青楼俄全盛遊 鳥刺し踊り」
中判校合摺　寛政2年（1790）頃
ボストン美術館所蔵

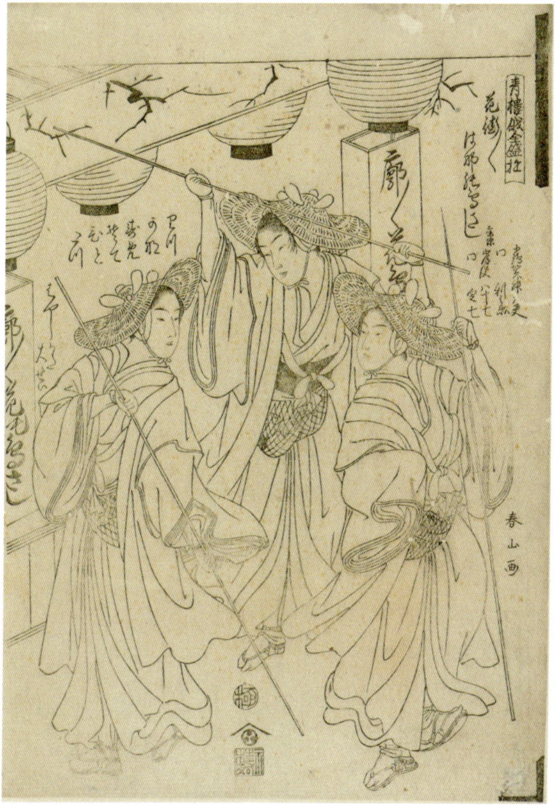

Katsukawa Shunzan, *Dance with Birding Poles*, from the series *Entertainments of the Niwaka Festival in the Yoshiwara in Full Swing*,
ca. 1790, *chuban kyogozuri*. Museum of Fine Arts, Boston.

©2024 Museum of Fine Arts, Boston. All rights reserved.
William S. and John T.Spaulding Collection,1921 21_4782

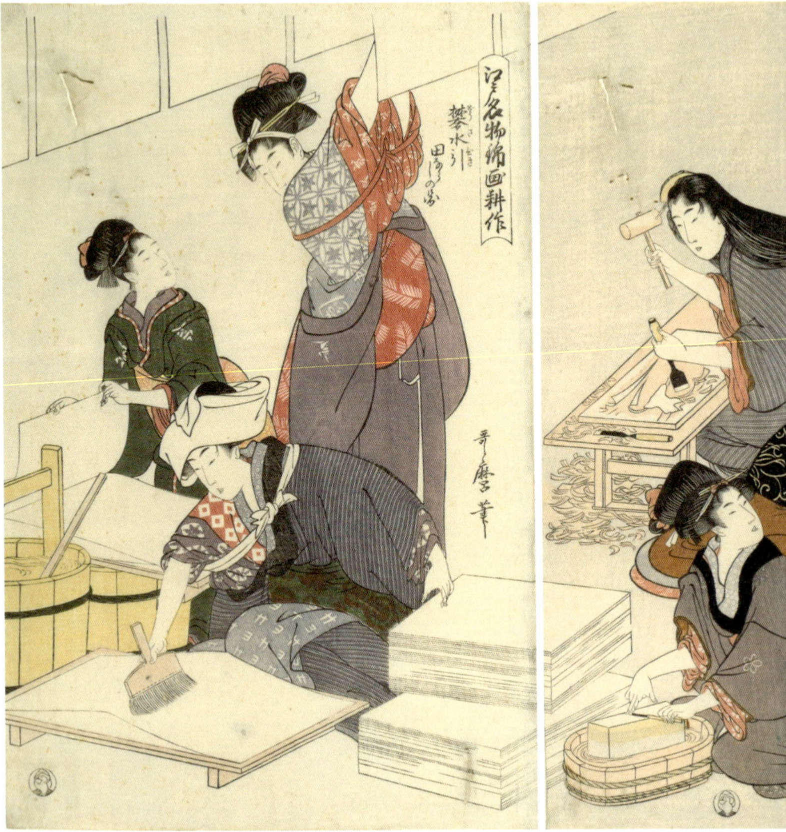

3.

Kitagawa Utamaro,
from the series *The Cultivation of Brocade Prints, a Famous Product of Edo*,
ca. 1803, *oban nishiki-e* triptych. The Art Institute of Chicago.

The production process of *nishiki-e*, depicted in the style of *bijinga* (lit. pictures of beautiful women). In reality the workforce at the time would have consisted mainly of men. From right to left, the triptych follows the process from 1. the artist's completion of the design; 2. the carving of the woodblocks; and 3. the preparation of the paper through a sizing technique known as *dosa-biki* (p. 105).

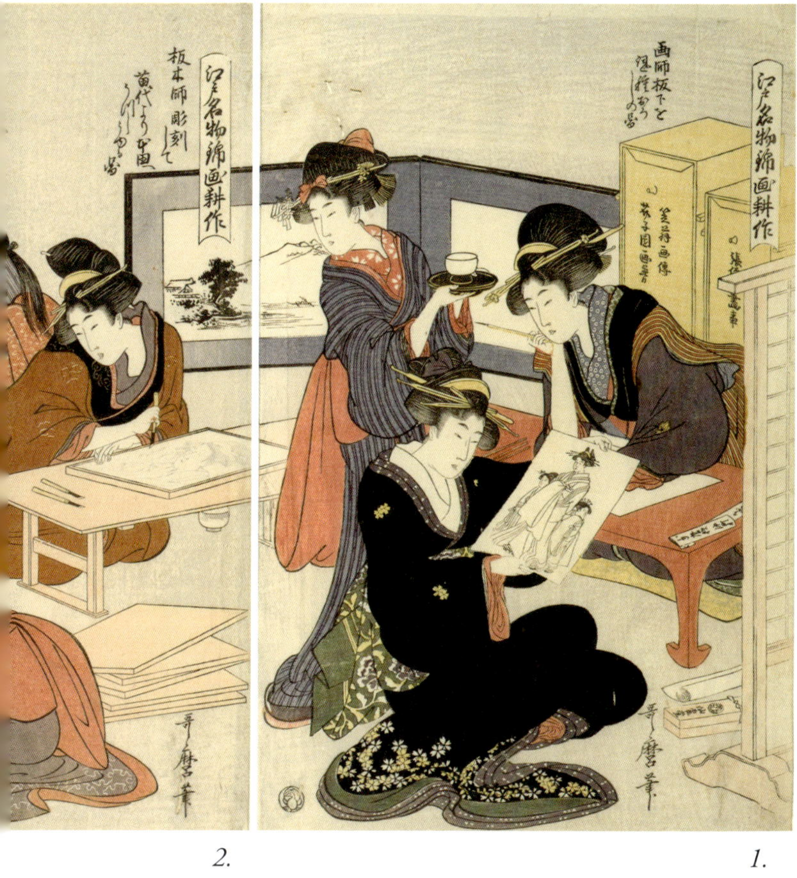

2.　　1.

喜多川歌麿「江戸名物錦画耕作」

大判錦絵３枚続　享和３年（1803）頃　シカゴ美術館所蔵
錦絵の制作工程を「美人画」の体裁で描いた作品で、実際には男性の職人が多いです。①絵師が版下絵を完成させたところから、②彫師の仕事、③紙の下処理作業（礬水引き p.105）までを描いています。

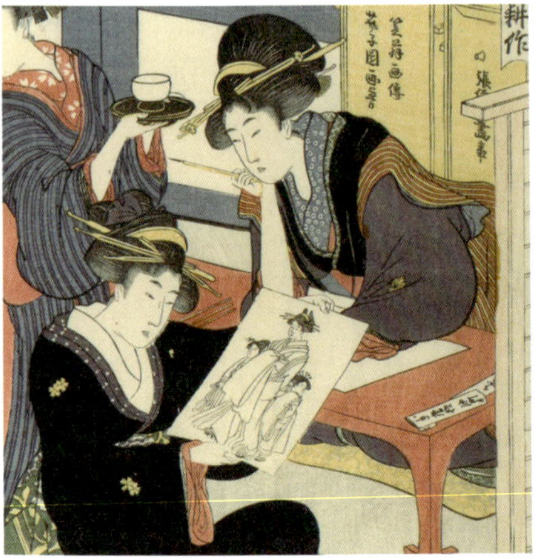

1.

The artist hands the design to the publisher. Artists principally used *sumi* ink in their work.

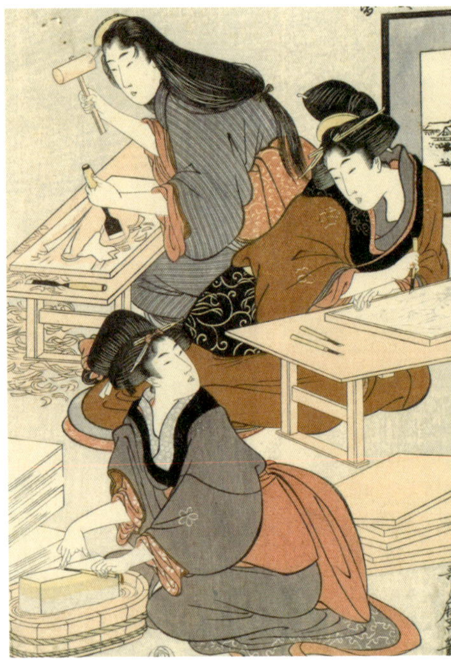

2.

The carver uses a *kogatana* (small knife) to cut the outlines of the design pasted face down onto the woodblock. Another uses a *nomi* (chisel) and *kizuchi* (wooden mallet) to even out the wider areas. In front, a girl sharpens carving tools.

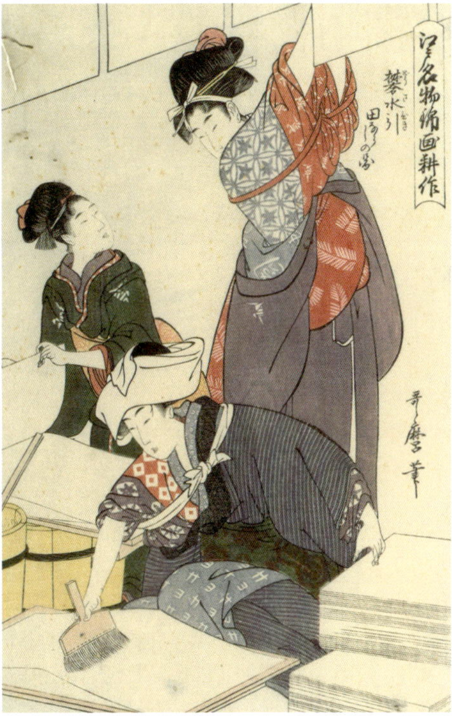

3.

To avoid color blotting during printing, the paper is treated with *dosa*, a solution of *nikawa* (animal glue) and *myoban* (alum), and dried.

①絵師が版下絵を版元の使いに渡しています。絵師は基本的に墨しか扱いません。

②版下絵を裏返しに貼り小刀で輪郭線を切り出す彫師と、線の周囲を大型の鑿と木槌で不要な部分を取り除いていく彫師。手前には彫刻刀を研ぐ娘がいます。

③絵の具の滲みを防ぐため、膠と明礬を混ぜた礬水を紙に塗り乾かす作業です。

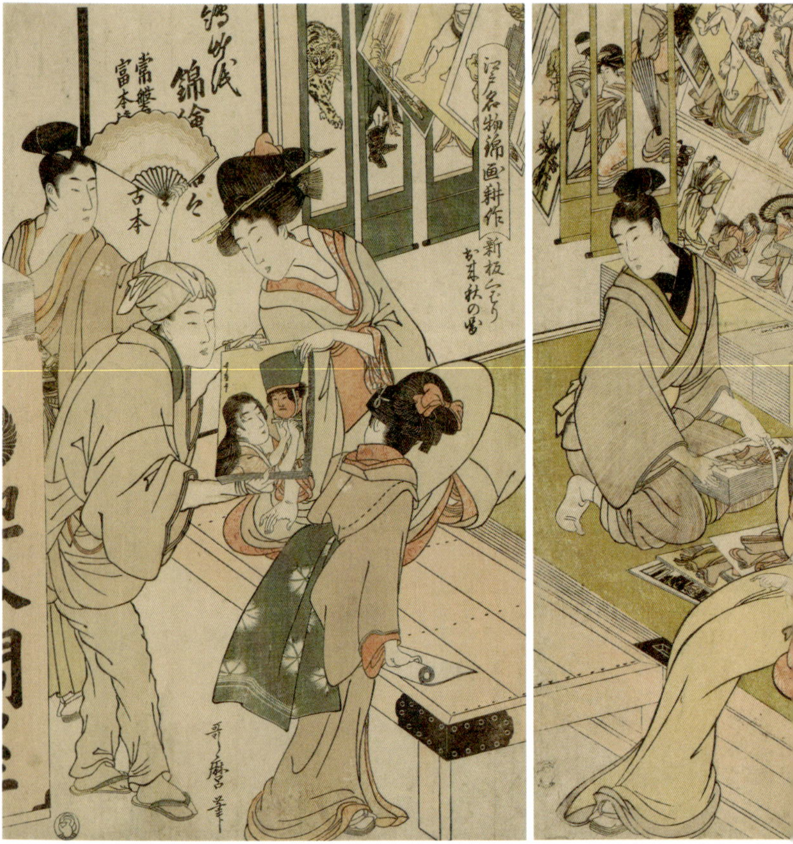

3.

Kitagawa Utamaro,
from the series *The Cultivation of Brocade Prints, a Famous Product of Edo*,
ca. 1803, *oban nishiki-e* triptych. The British Museum.

Continuing from the previous work (p. 18-21), this triptych depicts, from right to left: 1. printers at work; 2. the *nishiki-e* print wholesaler's storefront; and 3. customers gathered excitedly in front. As shown here, some publishers established a shop and sold directly to customers, while others would consign prints to small retailers.

 ©The Trustees of the British Museum c/o DNPartcom

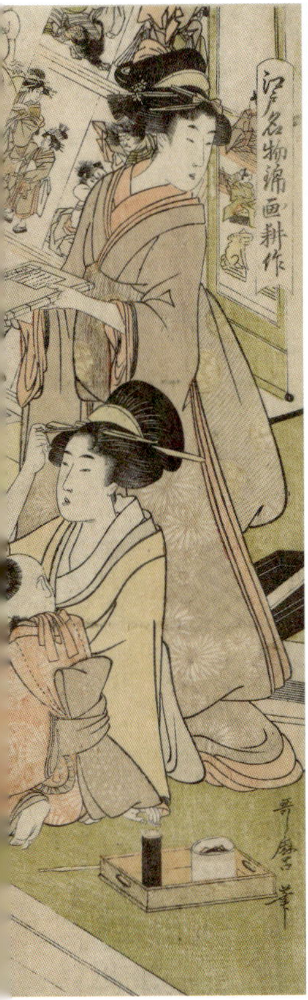

2.

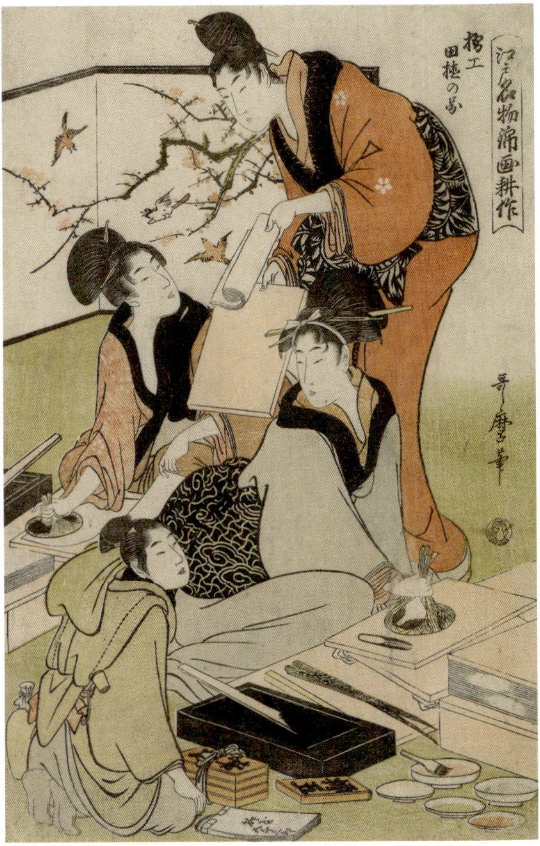

1.

喜多川歌麿「江戸名物錦画耕作」

大判錦絵3枚続　享和3年（1803）頃　大英博物館所蔵

前ページ（p.18-21）の作品の続きで、①摺師の仕事から、②錦絵販売の店先、③客の様子までを描いています。このように版元が店を構えて直接販売する場合と、小売の店に委託する場合があります。

1.

The publisher hands color-separated test prints and carved woodblocks to the printer, who holds a *baren* (p. 105). The printing stand is set at an angle, making it easier to apply pressure evenly with the *baren* during printing.

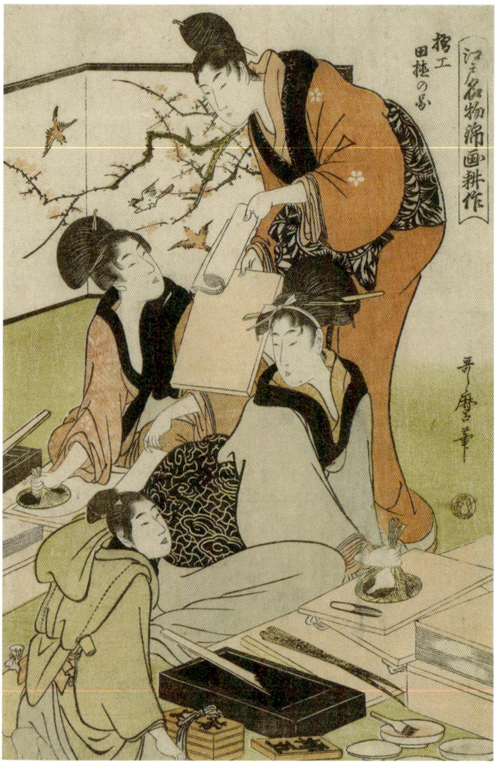

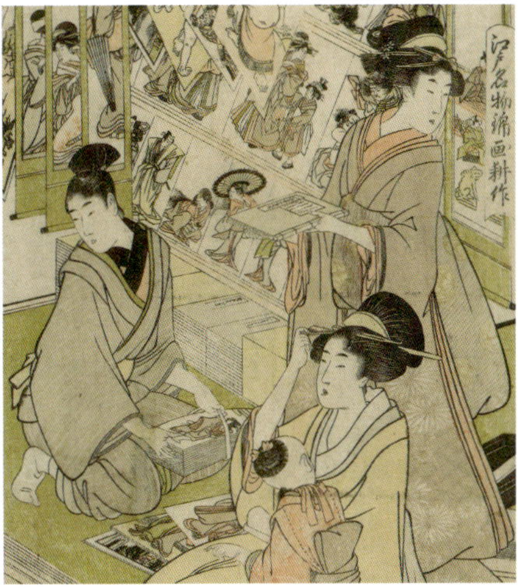

2.
Nishiki-e prints on display in the shop. Long, narrow prints known as *hashira-e* (lit. pillar pictures) hang for sale in the background, set upon simple mountings.

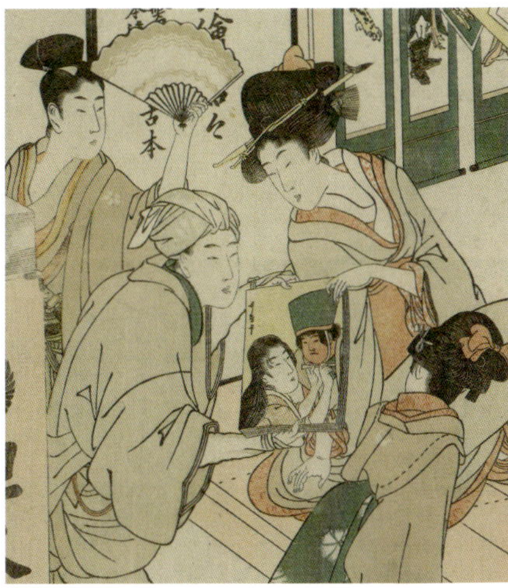

3.
A customer considers purchasing a ukiyo-e print featuring the folkloric figures of a *yamauba* (mountain witch) and the heroic Kintaro, a theme that was a specialty of Utamaro's.

①版元が、色指定をした校合摺と彫った版木を、バレン（p.105）を手にする摺師に渡しています。摺台は、均等に力がかかるように、斜めになっています。

②店に錦絵が並んでいます。柱絵と呼ばれる細長い画面の錦絵は、簡単な表装をして売られていました。

③客が錦絵を買おうとしています。歌麿が得意とした図柄で、昔話に出てくる山姥と金太郎です。

Utagawa Hiroshige, *Komagata Hall and Azuma Bridge*, from the series *One Hundred Famous Views of Edo*,
1857, *oban nishiki-e*. The Art Institute of Chicago.

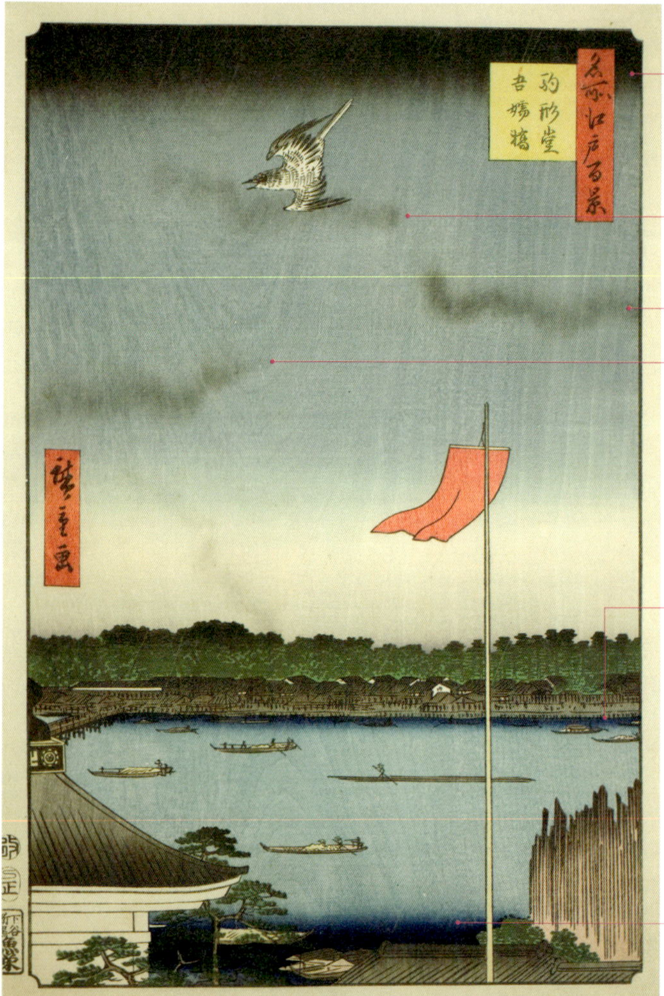

歌川広重「名所江戸百景　駒形堂吾妻橋」
大判錦絵　安政4年（1857）　シカゴ美術館所蔵

Special Techniques

A *nishiki-e* print is best appreciated in hand and examined finely, revealing the intricacies and ingenuity in the carving and printing process discernible only upon close inspection. Special techniques employed by the carver and printer, such as *karazuri* (lit. empty printing), *bokashi* (shading), and *kewari* (lit. hair-splitting) delighted viewers all the more.

● *Ate-nashi bokashi*

Ate-nashi bokashi, or indeterminate shading, is a gradation technique in which the target area is moistened with water, pigment applied, and the paper printed, producing a shaded color area of a natural shape that varies with each printing.

● *Fuki bokashi*

Fuki bokashi, or wiped shading, is a technique used to produce soft gradation that involves wiping the woodblock with a dampened cloth to moisten it, before applying pigment with a brush and printing. A printer's skill is vital to the execution of this technique.

特別な技法

手に持って眺めるのが、基本的な錦絵の鑑賞スタイルです。それだけに、目を近づけてこそ味わえる彫摺の工夫が随所に見られます。空摺、ぼかし、毛割など、彫師と摺師の特別な技法が、鑑賞者の目を一層楽しませていました。

●あてなしぼかし

ぼかす場所に水分を含ませ、そこに絵の具をたらし、自然な滲みを生かして摺るぼかし技法です。

●拭きぼかし

濡らした雑巾で板木を拭いて水を含ませ、刷毛で絵の具をはいてぼかす技法。摺師の腕がものをいいます。

Utagawa Toyokuni III,
The Actor Hikosaburo Bando V as Ono-no-Tofu,
1863, *oban nishiki-e.* Chiba City Museum of Art.

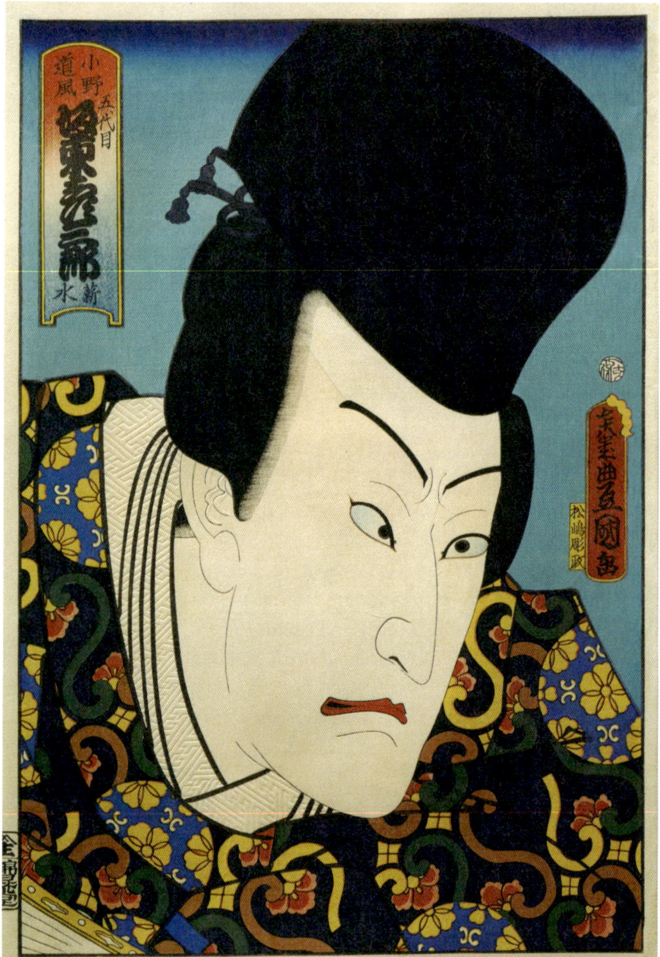

三代歌川豊国「五代目坂東彦三郎の小野道風」
大判錦絵　文久3年（1863）　千葉市美術館所蔵

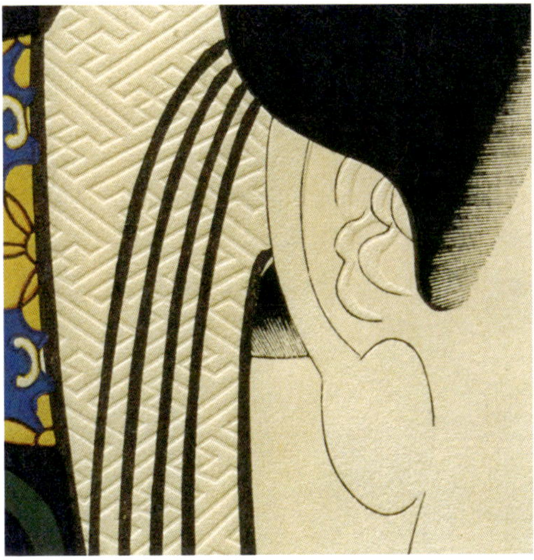

● *Karazuri*

Karazuri, or embossing, is a technique where paper is printed without applying pigment, using the unevenness of the woodblock to create shapes and textures. A further embossing technique known as *kimedashi* (lit. pressing out), used here for the ear section, involves printing forcefully onto a deeply carved block, thereby enhancing the three-dimensional effect.

●空摺

絵の具をつけずに摺り、凹凸で形や質感を表す技法です。特に深く彫った版木で強く摺り、立体感を高めた技法は「きめ出し」（耳の部分）と呼ばれます。

Utagawa Toyokuni III,
***The Actor Onoe Kikujiro II as Princess Takiyasha*,**
1862, *oban nishiki-e*. Chiba City Museum of Art.

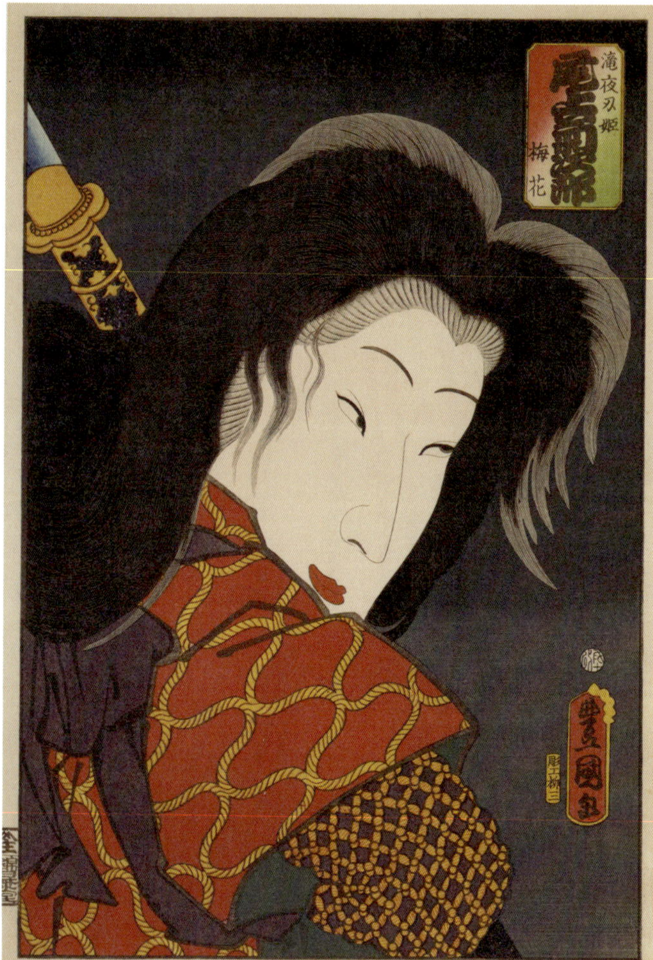

三代歌川豊国「二代目尾上菊次郎の滝夜叉姫」
大判錦絵　文久2年（1862）　千葉市美術館所蔵

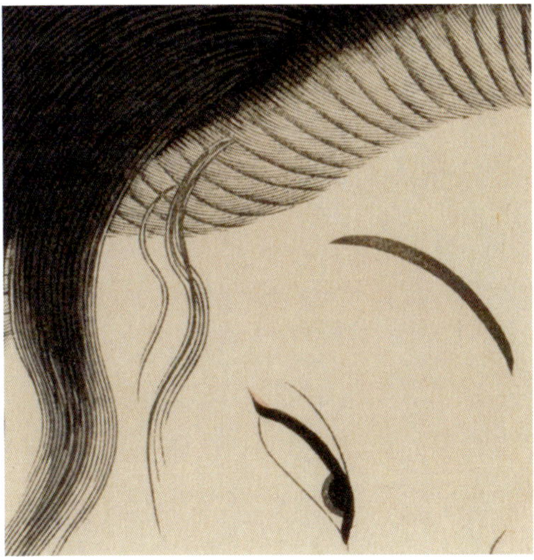

● ***Kewari***

Kewari is a highly advanced technique used to capture the individual hairs of the hairline, where skilled carvers might fit three strands of hair within a single millimeter. It is one of the salient features of *ookubi-e* (p. 106), in which the subject's face is enlarged for emphasis.

●毛割

１mmに３本の毛を彫ることのできる優れた彫師が生え際の毛を担当しました。顔を大きく描く「大首絵」(p.106) の見どころです。

Chapter 2

Everyday Life in Edo

第二章

江戸の日常

Embracing Life amid the City's Blessings

Ukiyo-e prints often capture the everyday moments in life, scenes familiar to all in that era. Their charm lies in elevating the commonplace into widely treasured works of art. From the mid-18th century, ukiyo-e began to frequently depict intimate interactions between both mothers and children, and playing children. Edo's well-developed infrastructure granted security, making children's healthy upbringing a point of pride among its residents. Celebrations like Hina Matsuri (Girls' Festival) and Tango no Sekku (Boys' Festival), once exclusive to the upper class, became widespread among common people and favored themes in ukiyo-e. Foreign visitors from the late Edo to Meiji periods often remarked upon the apparent happiness of Japanese children. These glimpses into the contented lives of ordinary people resonated deeply with viewers, evoking empathy and joy.

都市の恵まれた生活

浮世絵には、その時代であればどこにでも見かけられる、平凡な日常を描く作品が多くあります。見慣れた光景であるはずの日常が、ことさらに絵の主題となり、それを購入する大衆がいたという点にも、浮世絵の大きな特性があります。特に18世紀半ば以降は、母と子の触れ合いや遊ぶ子どもの姿が多く浮世絵に描かれるようになりました。インフラの整った都市の恩恵により安心して生活ができ、子どもが健康に育つということは、「将軍様のお膝元」である江戸に住む町人たちにとって誇りでもありました。江戸時代より前には上流階級の間で行われていたような上巳（ひな祭り）や端午の節句といった子どもの成長を祝う行事が、庶民にまで普及するようになり、浮世絵の格好の主題ともなりました。実際、幕末から明治に来日した外国人の多くが、日本の子どもが幸せそうにしている様子を印象深く書き残しています。名もない庶民の満たされた生活の光景に、浮世絵の鑑賞者も親しく共感し幸福感を得ていたのでしょう。

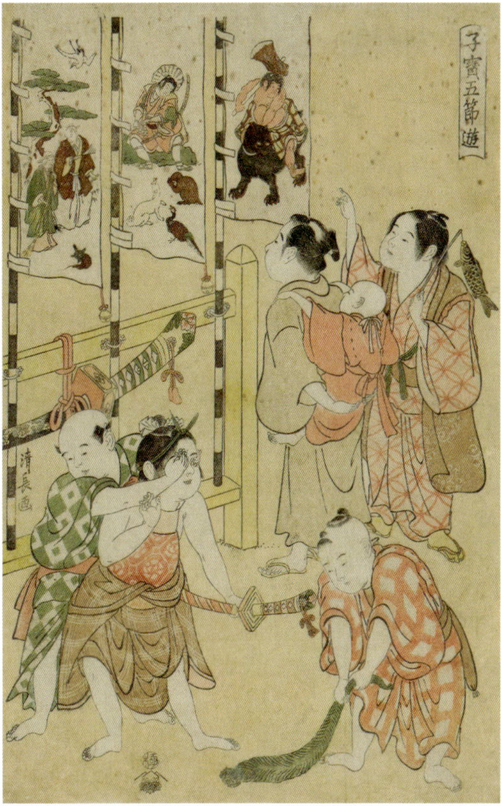

Torii Kiyonaga, *The Boys' Festival*,
from the series *Precious Children's Games of the Five Festivals*,
ca. 1794-95, *oban nishiki-e*. Suntory Museum of Art.

Boys' Day is a festival celebrating boys' growth and maturation, where displays of banners and weaponry symbolize strength and success in battle. The tradition of flying carp streamers as a symbol of aspiration for success is still observed in many places today.

鳥居清長「子宝五節遊　端午」
大判錦絵　寛政6-7年（1794-95）頃
サントリー美術館所蔵
端午の節句は、男の子の成長を祝う行事で、たくましさや武運を願う幟や武具が飾られます。出世の象徴の鯉のぼりを飾る習慣は、現在でも各地に見られます。

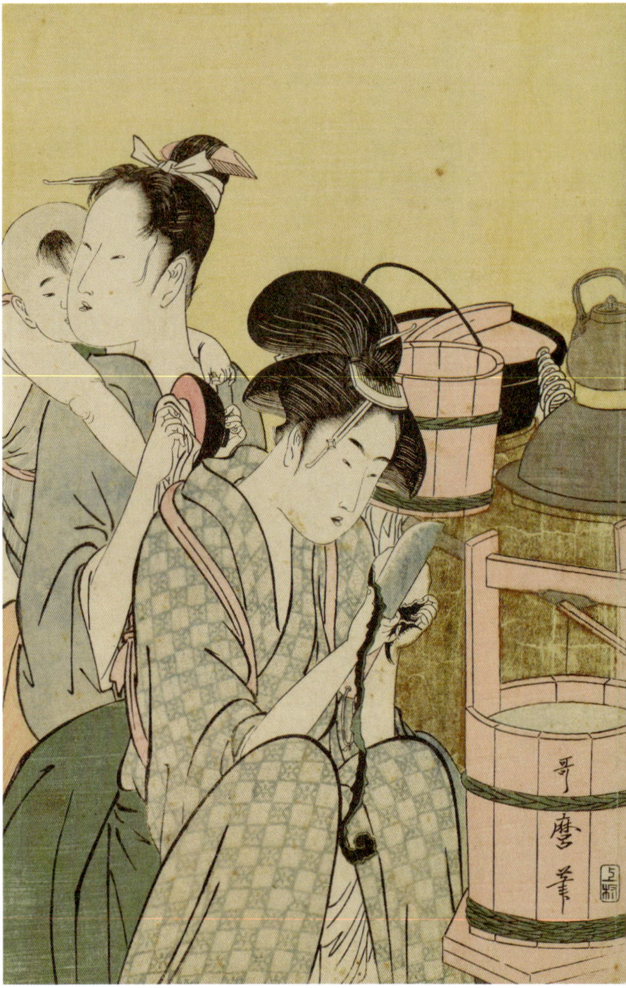

Kitagawa Utamaro, *Kitchen Scene*,
1794-95, *oban nishiki-e* diptych. Tokyo National Museum.

Women prepare a meal around a traditional *kamado* stove. One lights the fire with a *takezutsu* (bamboo tube) as another peels vegetables, and a mother wipes dishes while soothing her baby.

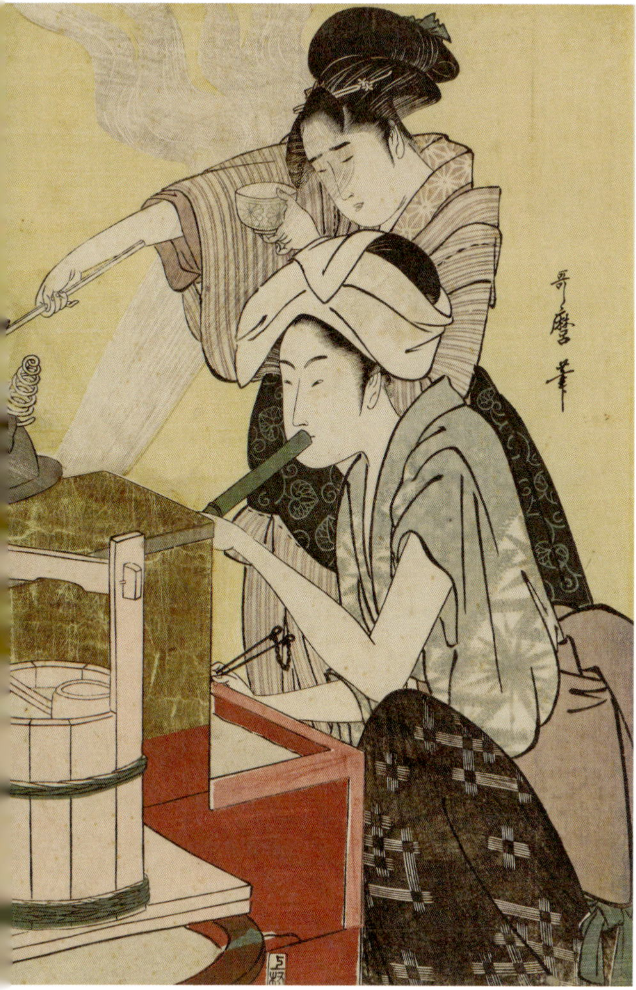

喜多川歌麿「台所」
大判錦絵２枚続　寛政6-7年（1794-95）
東京国立博物館所蔵
かまどを囲んで料理の準備をする女たちです。竹筒で火をおこしたり、野菜の皮をむいたり、食器を拭きながら赤ん坊をあやす母親もいます。

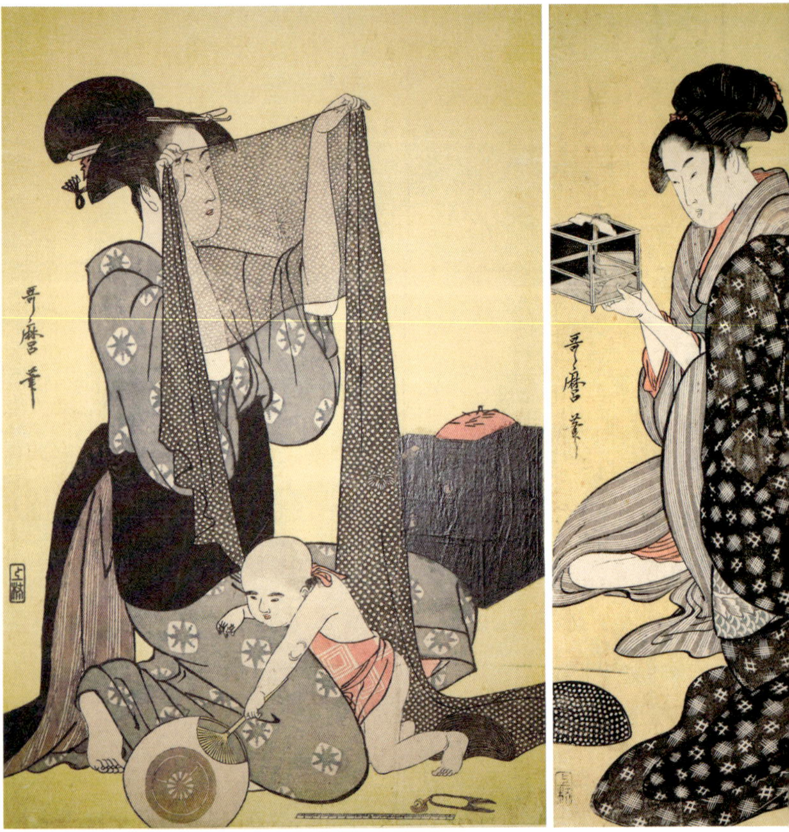

Kitagawa Utamaro, *Women Examining Pieces of Cloth Preparatory to Making Garments,*
ca. 1794-95, *oban nishiki-e* triptych. The New York Public Library.

Women spread out fabrics to prepare for sewing. Around them, a baby seeks attention, a boy teases a cat with a mirror, and a girl peers into an insect cage.

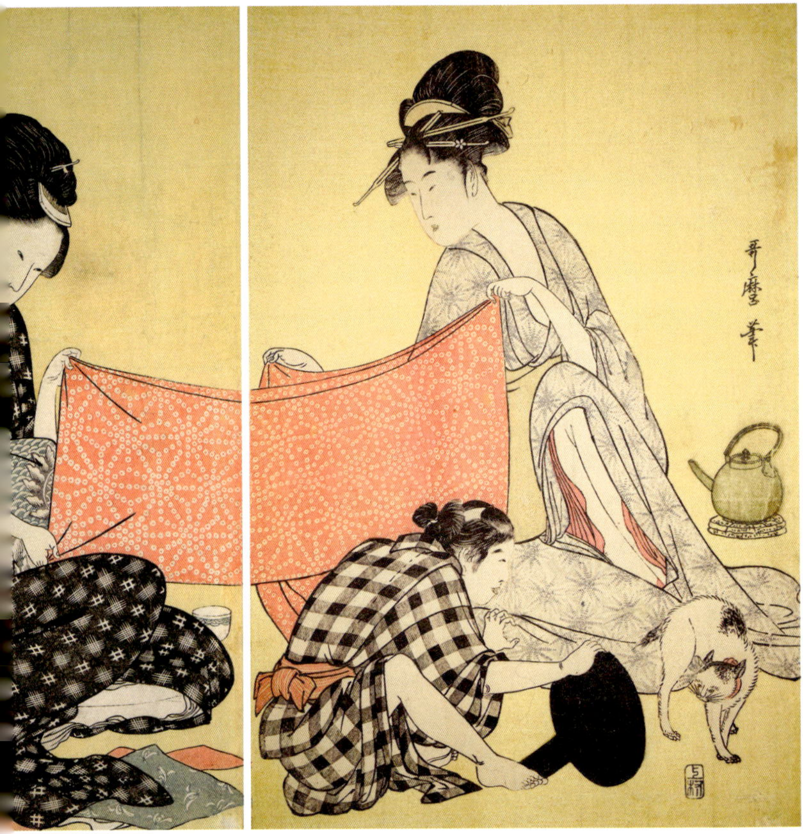

喜多川歌麿「針仕事」
大判錦絵3枚続　寛政6-7年（1794-95）
ニューヨーク公共図書館所蔵
布を広げて裁縫の準備をする女たち。その周りでは、甘える赤ん坊や、猫を鏡でからかう男の子、虫籠を覗く娘なども描き込まれています。

Chapter 3

Landscape

第三章

風景

From Edo to the Provinces

Before the Edo period, when Kyoto was the epicenter of Japan, Edo was seen as a distant, unremarkable outpost. But with the onset of the Edo period, its residents began to discover and develop their own landmarks. Utagawa Hiroshige's series *One Hundred Famous Views of Edo*, compiled at the close of the Edo period, stands as ukiyo-e's finest tribute to Edo's famous sights. Nihonbashi, a bridge arching over the canal between Edo Castle's outer moat and the Sumida River, eventually gave its name to the vibrant surrounding fish-market district. The shogunate's extensive network of waterways and the Sumida River's abundant flow endowed Edo with a beautiful landscape, earning it the moniker of "the city of water." Nihonbashi was also the origin of the famous *Gokaido* (p. 107), whose development made travel a tangible dream for its residents.

江戸から諸国へ

京都が日本の中心だった江戸時代より前には、知られた名所もない寂しい場所というのが江戸のイメージでした。しかし開府以来、この新しい都市に暮らす人々は、無数の名所を見出し誕生させてきたのです。浮世絵における江戸名所の集大成が、幕末にまとめられた歌川広重の「名所江戸百景」のシリーズです。江戸城の外堀と隅田川を結ぶ水路に架けられた「日本橋」は、やがて魚河岸もあったその繁華な地域一帯を示す地名ともなりましたが、幕府によって整備された多くの水路と豊かな水流の隅田川によって、江戸は水の都ともいえるような美しい景観を備えました。また日本橋は五街道（p.107）の起点でもあり、街道の整備も行き届いていく中で、町人にとっても旅は現実的な憧れになっていきます。

葛飾北斎が「冨嶽三十六景」、歌川広重が「東海道五拾三次之内」のシリーズを

In the Tempo era (1830-44), the remarkable popularity of Katsushika Hokusai's *Thirty-six Views of Mount Fuji* and Utagawa Hiroshige's *Fifty-three Stations of the Tokaido* series established the landscape print genre in ukiyo-e. Their prints sparked a surge of interest in the provinces, prompting journeys to see Mount Fuji, explore Enoshima and Ise, and savor regional delicacies along the highways.

At the same time, the introduction of "Prussian blue" (also known as "Berlin blue"), a chemically synthesized pigment with a strong tint, greatly advanced landscape painting in Japan, enabling the creation of beautiful gradations and the expression of expansive spaces. Hokusai's *Thirty-six Views of Mount Fuji* is a milestone work marking the introduction of the pigment. Another artist who made effective use of this distinctive color was Hiroshige, to such an extent that it later came to be known in the West as "Hiroshige blue."

ヒットさせ、本格的に浮世絵に風景画というジャンルを確立したのは、天保期（1830-44）のことでした。江戸から遠くに見えていた富士山を間近に見たい、江の島や伊勢に詣でたい、街道の宿場ごとに地方の名物を味わってみたいなど、このような風景画が地方への関心をさらに誘発したのは間違いありません。

この時代には、伸びの良い青色の化学染料の絵の具「プルシアンブルー（ベロ藍）」が日本にもたらされたことも風景画を大きく発展させました。美しいぼかし摺が可能になり、空間の広がりが表現されるようになります。この絵の具の導入による記念碑的な作品が、北斎の「冨嶽三十六景」であり、また広重はこの色を効果的に用いて、後世に西洋では「ヒロシゲ・ブルー」として記憶されることになります。

Edo

Utagawa Hiroshige, *Nihonbashi Bridge: Clearing after Snow*, from the series *One Hundred Famous Views of Edo*,
1856, *oban nishiki-e*. The Art Institute of Chicago.

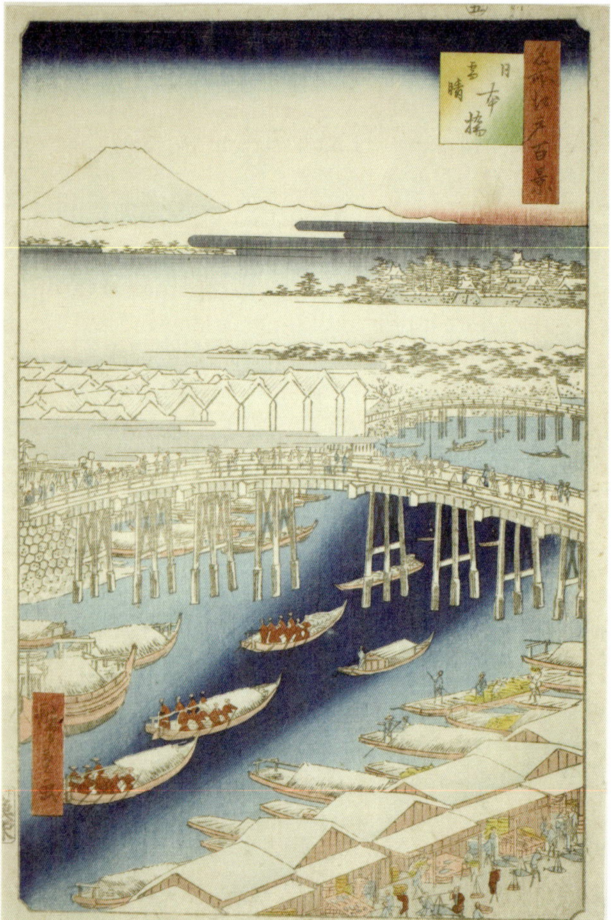

歌川広重「名所江戸百景　日本橋雪晴」
大判錦絵　安政３年（1856）　シカゴ美術館所蔵

Utagawa Hiroshige, *Kinryuzan Temple at Asakusa*, from the series *One Hundred Famous Views of Edo*,
1856, *oban nishiki-e*. The Metropolitan Museum of Art.

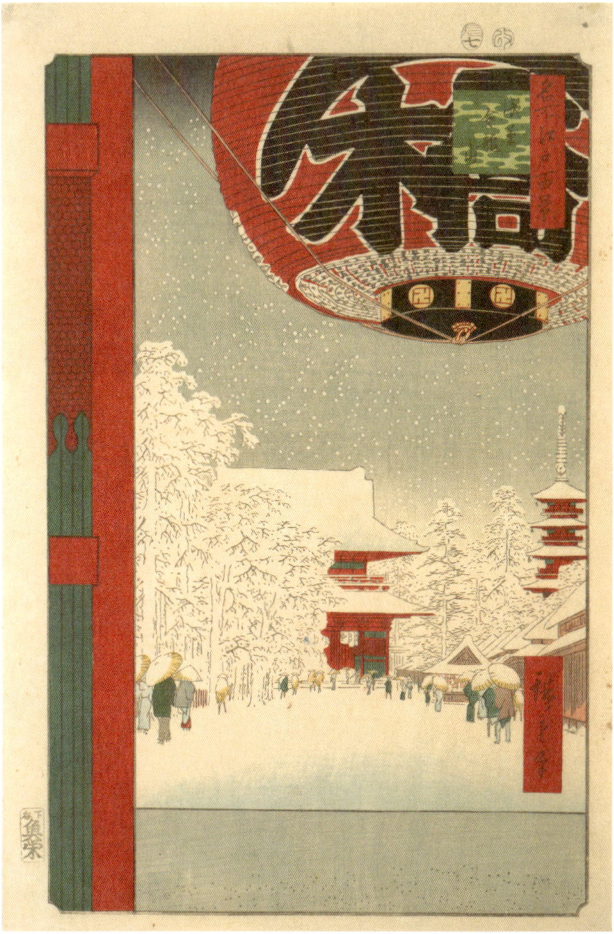

歌川広重「名所江戸百景　浅草金龍山」
大判錦絵　安政３年（1856）メトロポリタン美術館所蔵

Utagawa Hiroshige, *Kiyomizu Hall and Shinobazu Pond at Ueno*, from the series *One Hundred Famous Views of Edo*,
1856, *oban nishiki-e*. The Art Institute of Chicago.

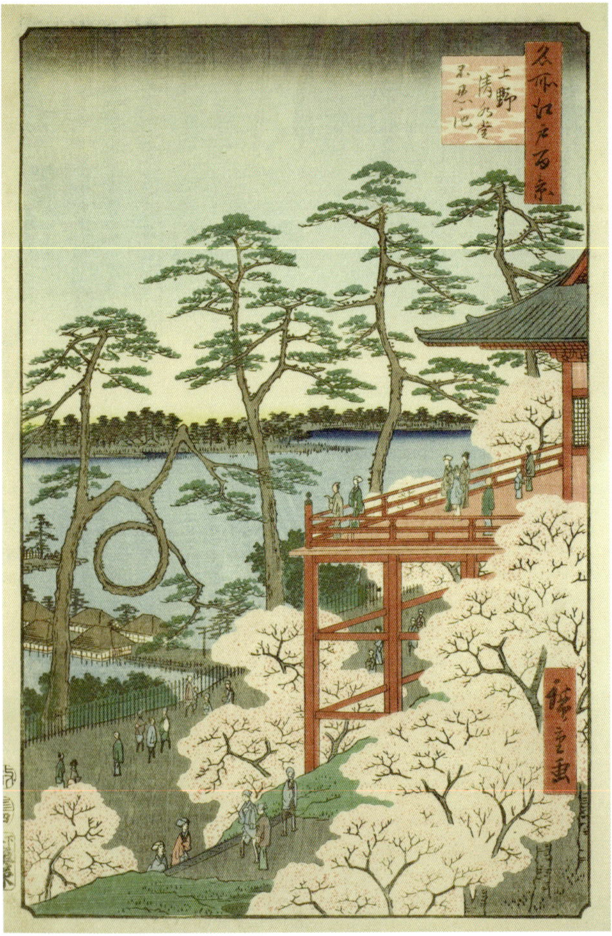

歌川広重「名所江戸百景　上野清水堂不忍ノ池」
大判錦絵　安政3年（1856）シカゴ美術館所蔵

Utagawa Hiroshige, *Sudden Shower over Shin-Ohashi Bridge and Atake*,
from the series *One Hundred Famous Views of Edo*,
1857, *oban nishiki-e*. The Metropolitan Museum of Art.

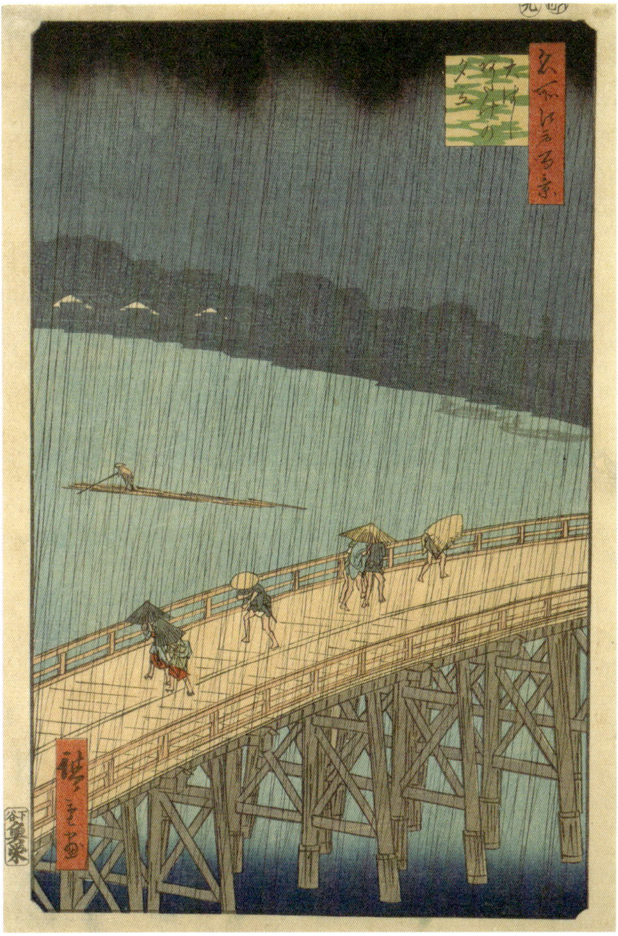

歌川広重「名所江戸百景　大はしあたけの夕立」
大判錦絵　安政４年（1857）　メトロポリタン美術館所蔵

Enoshima

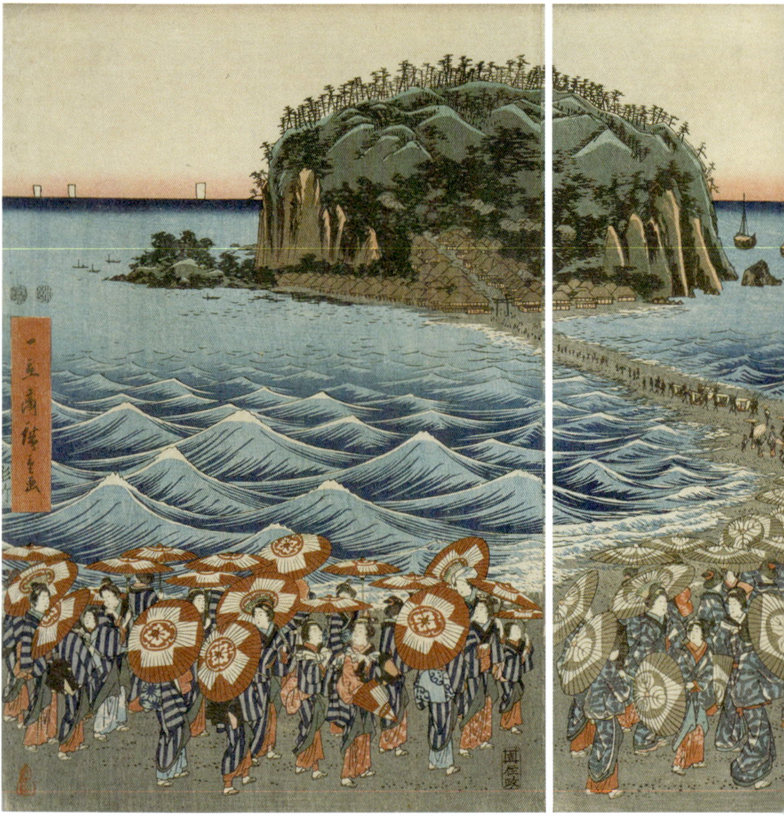

Utagawa Hiroshige, *Pilgrimage to the Shrine of Benzaiten at Enoshima in Sagami Province*,
1851, *oban nishiki-e* triptych.
Kanagawa Prefectural Museum of Cultural History.

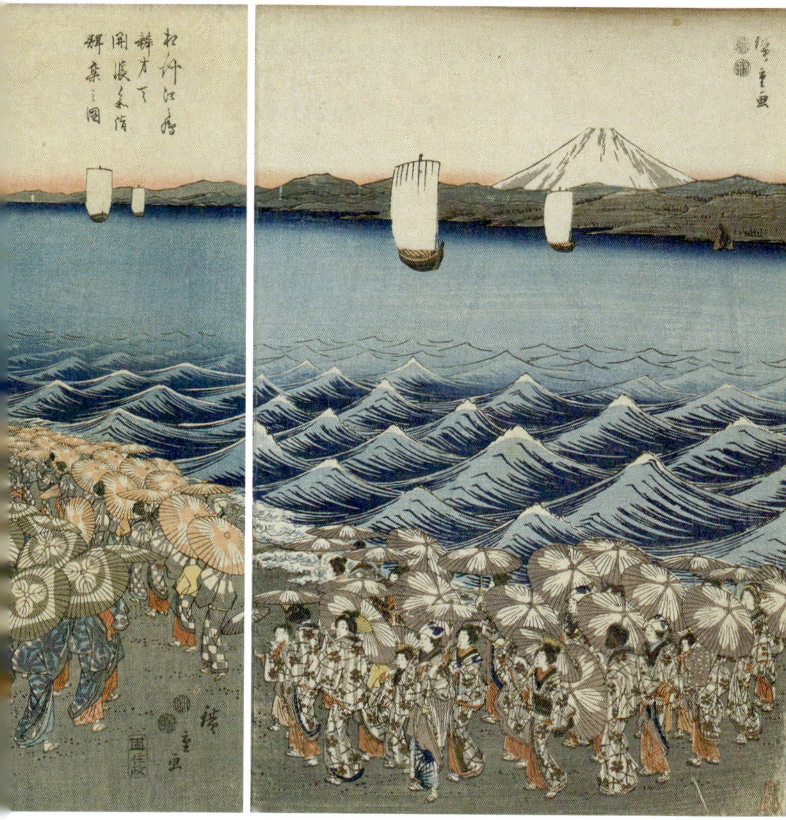

歌川広重「相州江之島弁才天開帳参詣群集之図」
大判錦絵3枚続　嘉永4年（1851）
神奈川県立歴史博物館所蔵

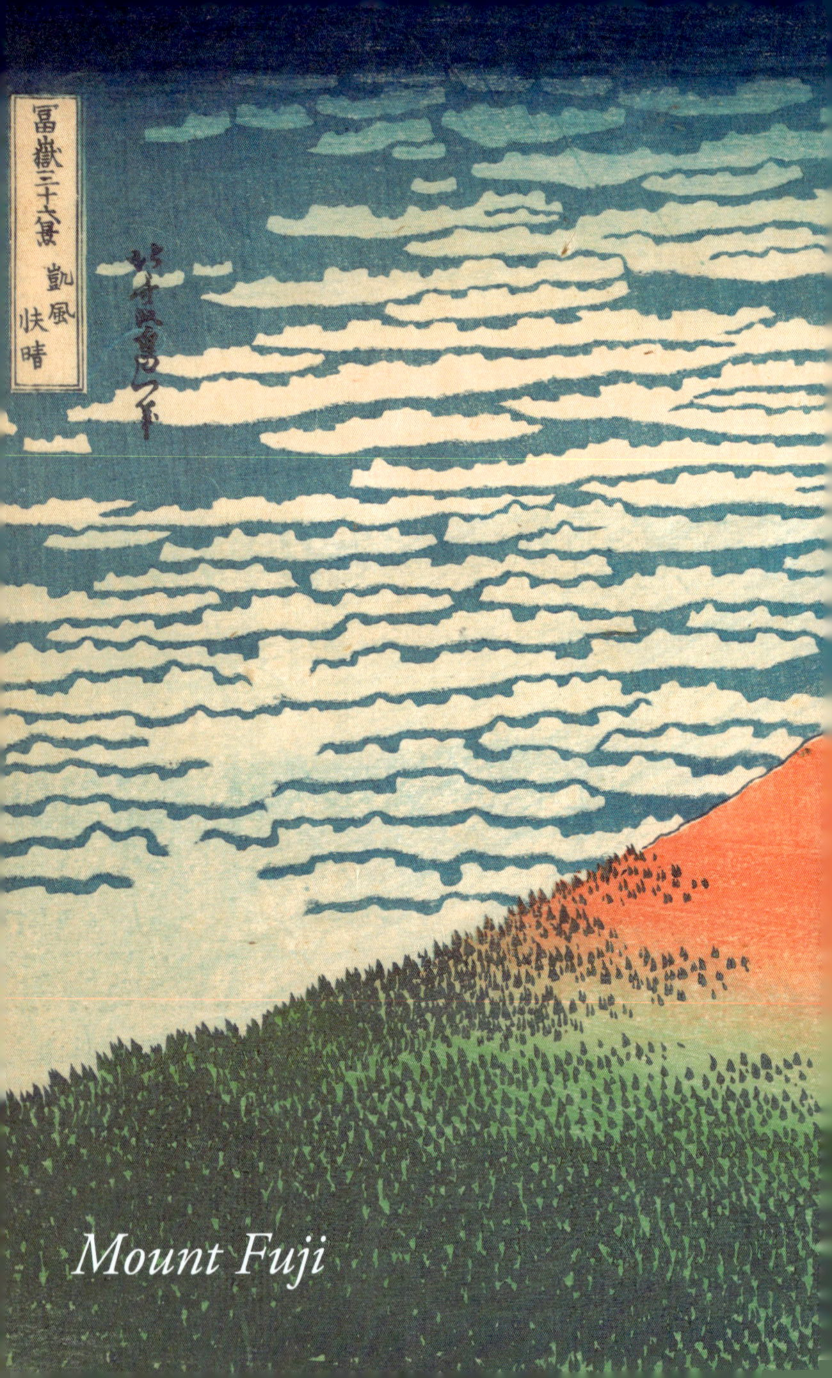

Mount Fuji

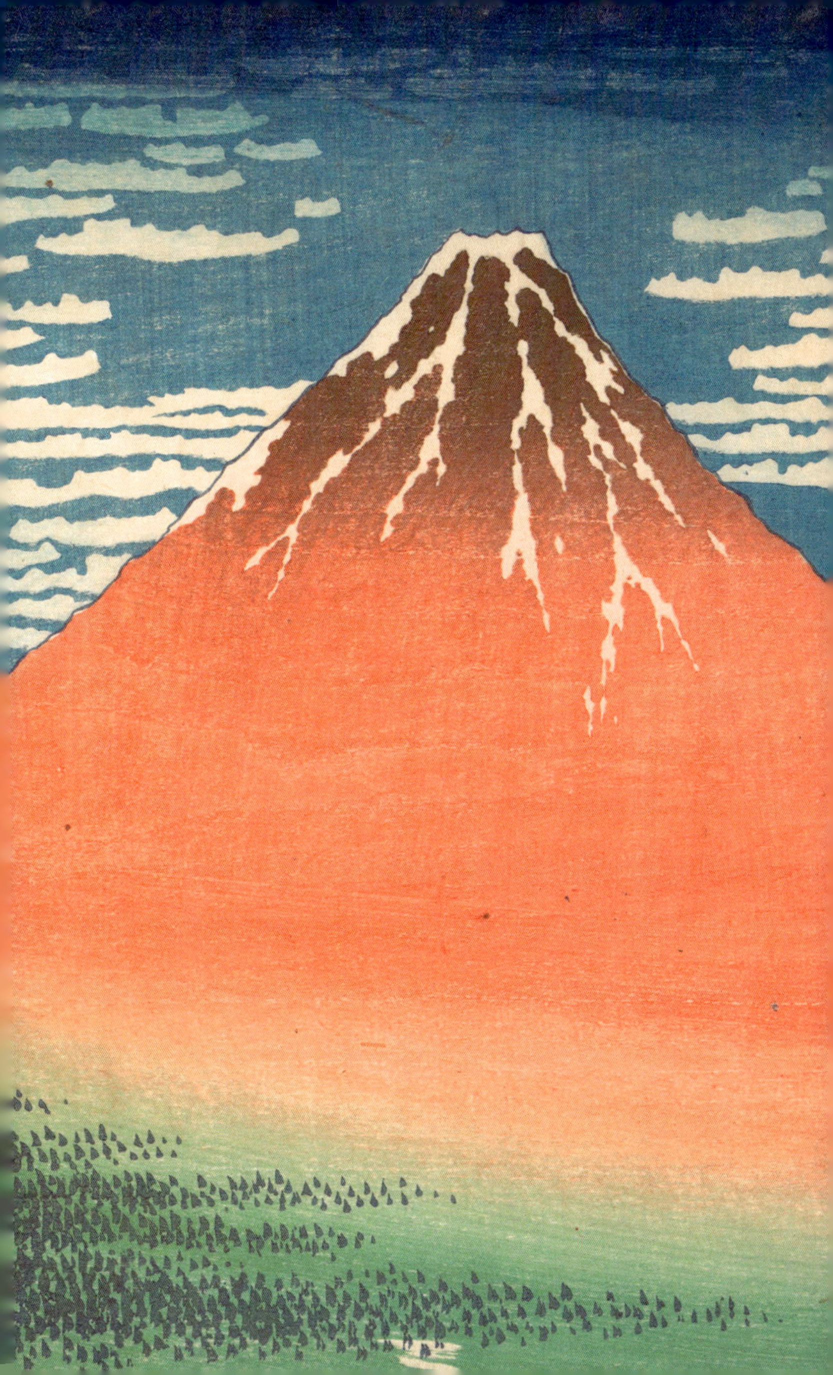

Hakone

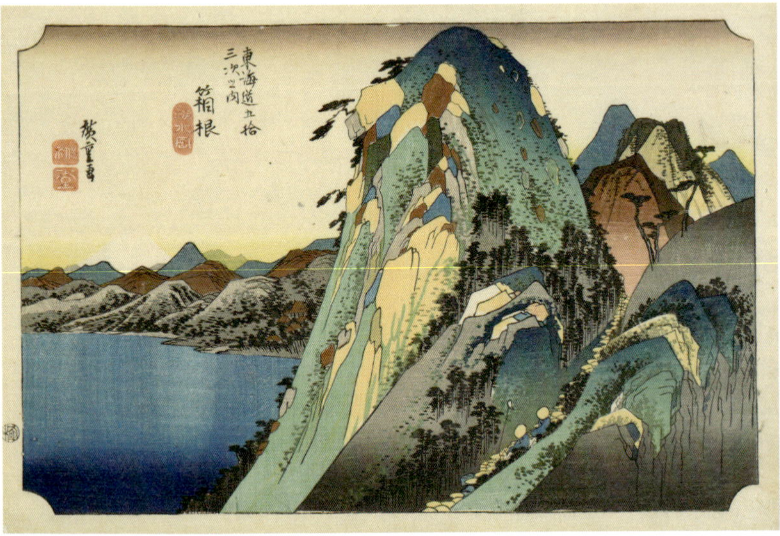

Utagawa Hiroshige, *Hakone: Lake Contours*, from the series *Fifty-three Stations of the Tokaido*,
ca. 1834-36, *oban nishiki-e*.
Shinjo Collection, Shimane Art Museum.

〈前ページ〉

Mount Fuji

Katsushika Hokusai, *South Wind, Clear Sky*, from the series *Thirty-six Views of Mount Fuji*,
ca. 1831-33, *oban nishiki-e*.
The Metropolitan Museum of Art.

葛飾北斎「冨嶽三十六景　凱風快晴」
大判錦絵　天保2-4年（1831-33）頃
メトロポリタン美術館所蔵

Inuyama Castle

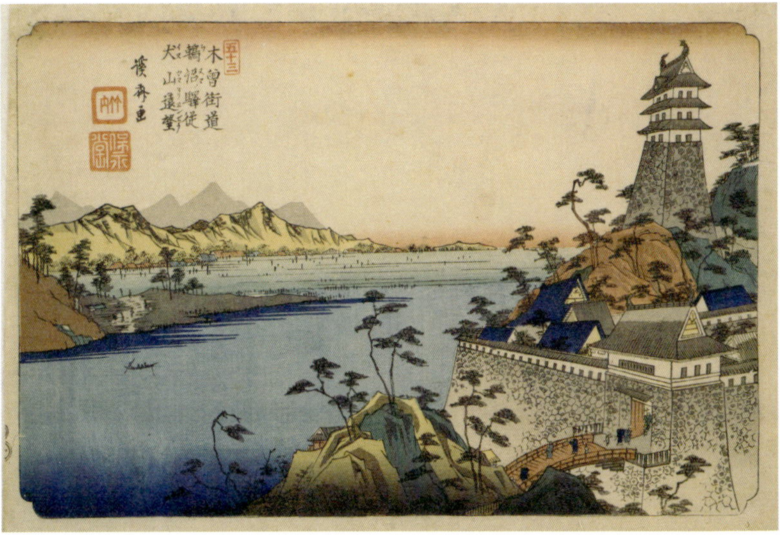

Keisai Eisen, *No. 53, Unuma Station: Distant View of Inuyama Castle*,
from the series *The Kisokaido*,
ca. 1835-36, *oban nishiki-e.*
Chiba City Museum of Art.

左／**歌川広重「東海道五拾三次之内　箱根　湖水図」**
大判錦絵　天保5-7年（1834-36）頃
島根県立美術館所蔵（新庄コレクション）
右／**渓斎英泉「五十三　木曽街道　鵜沼駅従犬山遠望」**
大判錦絵　天保6-7年（1835-36）頃　千葉市美術館所蔵

Kyoto

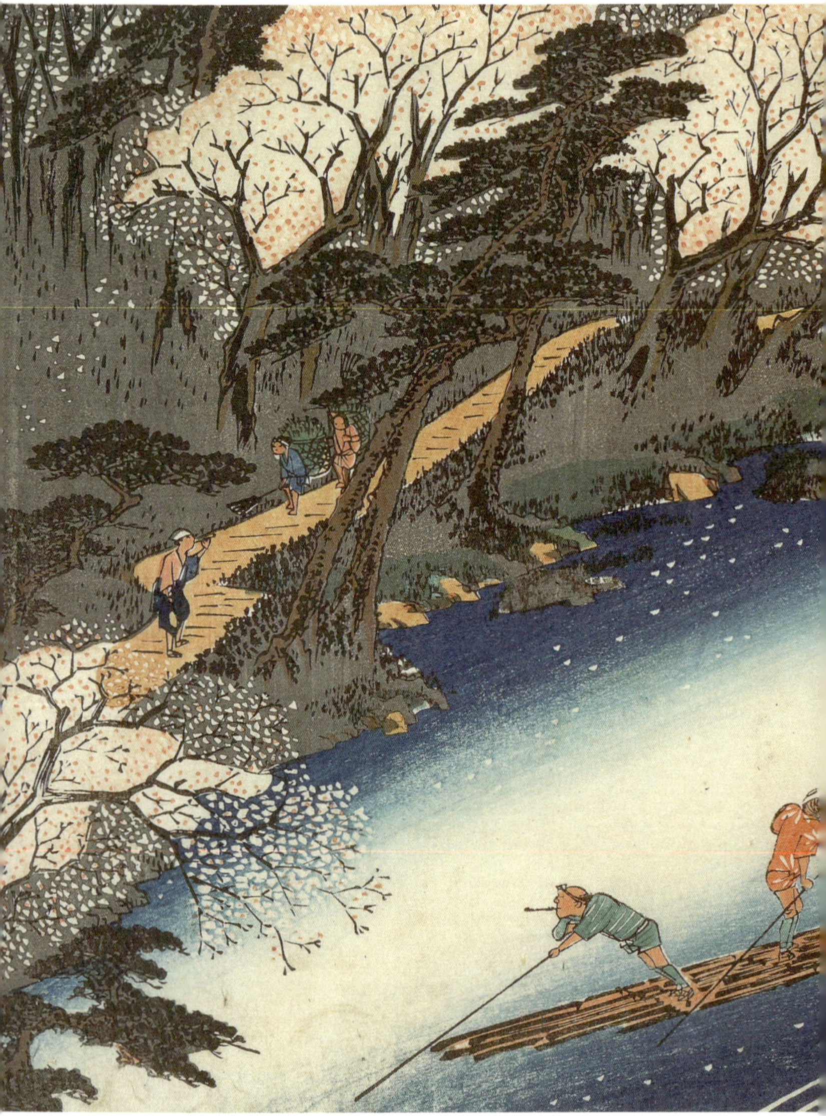

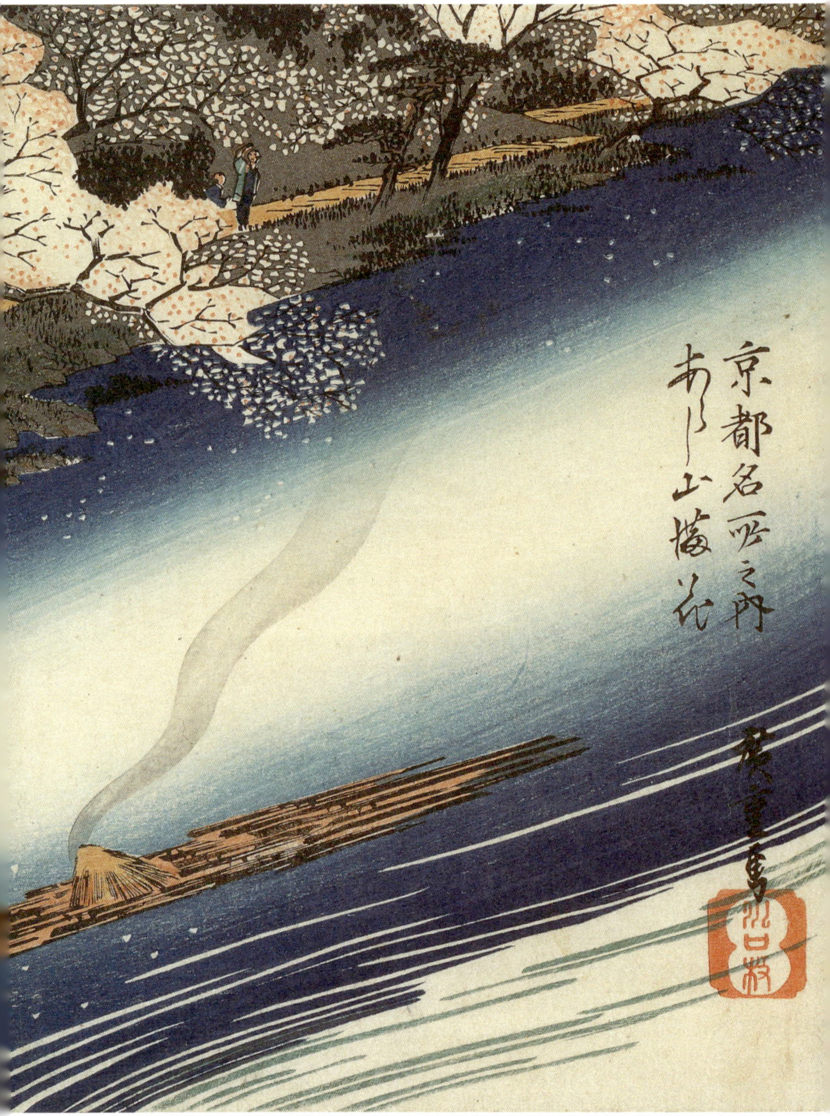
京都名所之内
あらし山満花
広重画

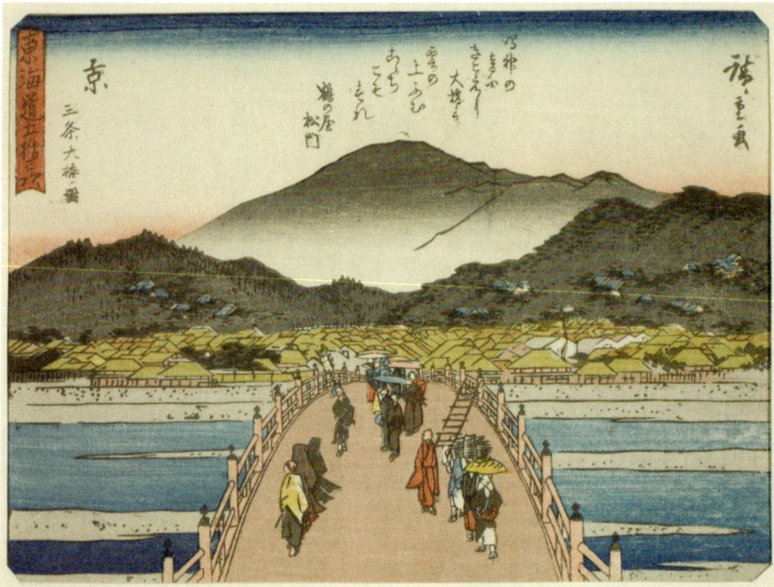

Utagawa Hiroshige, *Kyoto: The Great Bridge at Sanjo*,
from the series *Fifty-three Stations of the Tokaido with Poem*,
ca. 1840-42, *koban nishiki-e.*
The Art Institute of Chicago.

〈前ページ〉

Kyoto

Utagawa Hiroshige, *Cherry Blossoms at Arashiyama*,
from the series *Famous Places of Kyoto*,
ca. 1834, *oban nishiki-e.* Hagi Uragami Museum.

歌川広重
「京都名所之内　あらし山満花」
大判錦絵　天保5年（1834）頃
山口県立萩美術館・浦上記念館所蔵

Utagawa Hiroshige, *Kiyomizu Temple*,
from the series *Famous Places of Kyoto*,
ca. 1834, *oban nishiki-e*. The Metropolitan Museum of Art.

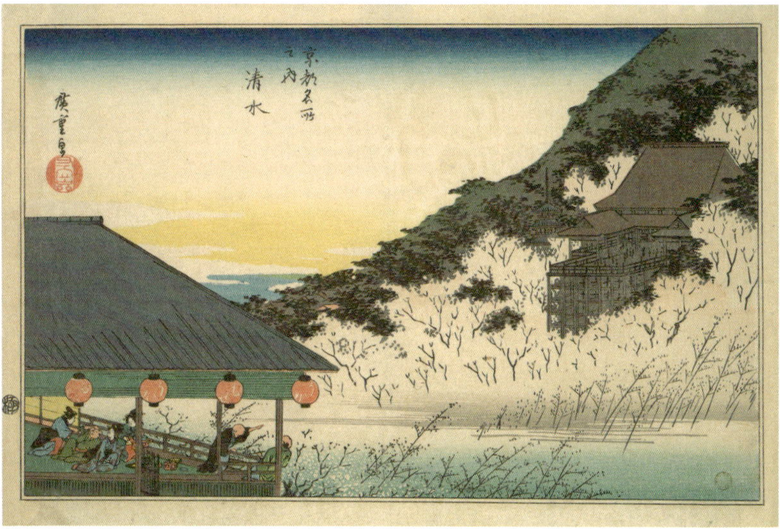

左／**歌川広重「狂歌入東海道五拾三次　京　三条大橋ノ図」**
小判錦絵　天保後期（1840-42）　シカゴ美術館所蔵
右／**歌川広重「京都名所之内　清水」**
大判錦絵　天保5年（1834）頃　メトロポリタン美術館所蔵

Chapter 4

Food

第四章

食

Timeless Edo Delicacies

Ukiyo-e's popularity lay in its depiction of contemporary trends and interests, yet it was not until the 19th century that food became prominent in its artworks. Before then, even when food was depicted, it lacked detailed representation or emphasis on specific cuisines.

Several factors might explain ukiyo-e's late Edo-period shift towards food as a subject. By that time, three daily meals had become customary, seasonings had advanced, and regional exchange was flourishing along with the food culture. The general populace began to embrace and enjoy food—nowhere more so than in the capital, where the Nihonbashi market became a converging point for a wide array of regional ingredients, diversifying Edo's culinary landscape to include everything from gourmet restaurant dishes to casual street food.

今も愛される江戸グルメ

浮世絵は、その時代ごとの流行や人々の関心事を積極的に主題とすることによって大衆の支持を得ていましたが、食への興味が現れるのは意外と遅く、19世紀に入ってからのことでした。それまでは、絵の中に料理の皿が並んで描かれていたとしても、どのような料理であるのか具体的に描き出そうという意識は薄かったようです。

幕末の浮世絵に食が多く主題として扱われるようになったのにはさまざまな理由があったと思いますが、日に3度の食事が普通になって久しく、調味料が発達し、地方との物の往来が活発化したことなどが食文化の興隆を促進したことは確かでしょう。

The emergence of *izakaya* (informal bars) around the city marked another transformation, giving rise to a phrase that captures the spirit of the time: “Kyoto for clothing, Osaka for eating, and Edo for drinking.” With Edo’s culinary prowess reaching new heights, some establishments expanded as far as the Kansai region. By the middle of the Edo period, the production of soy sauce, once reliant on Kansai, began in the Kanto region, further enriching Edo’s culinary repertoire. *Nigiri* sushi, soba noodles, tempura, *kabayaki* (grilled eel)—these timeless delicacies, favourites to this day, all originated in this vibrant era.

一般庶民に至るまで食を楽しみ、関心を持つ時代が到来したのです。特に江戸には、日本橋を中心にさまざまな食材が地方からもたらされ、料亭の高級料理から屋台で気軽に食べられるような庶民の料理まで、食は多様化していきました。

居酒屋ができたのも同じ頃のようで、当時は「京の着倒れ　大坂の食い倒れ　江戸の呑み倒れ」などと言われました。江戸の料理屋の実力も上がり、上方に進出することもあったようです。江戸時代中期には、上方に頼っていた醤油が関東でも生産されるようになったことも料理の幅を広げました。現在も多くの人に愛される握り寿司、蕎麦、天ぷら、鰻の蒲焼きなどは、この時代に生まれた江戸グルメです。

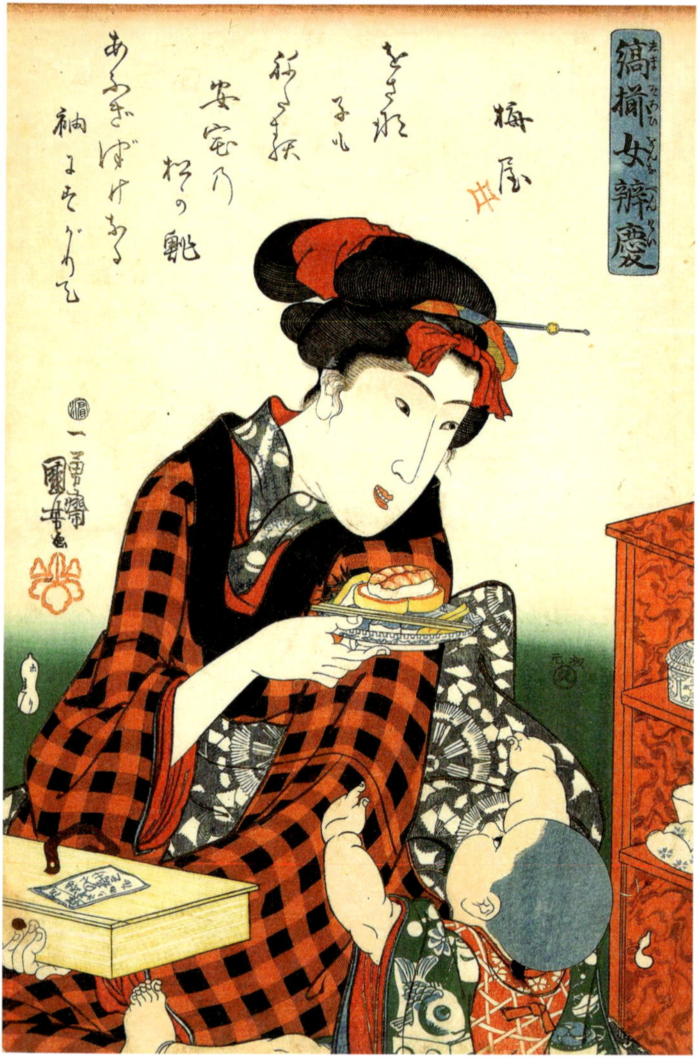
縞揃女辨慶
一勇齋國芳画

Sushi

Utagawa Kuniyoshi, *Takeout Sushi Parodying "The Pine of Ataka,"* from the series *Women in Benkei-checked Fabrics,*
1844, *oban nishiki-e*. Tokyo Metropolitan Library.

A child begs for a plate of *nigiri* sushi in a humorous parody of a scene from the kabuki play "The Pine of Ataka." The sushi box label reads "Matsu no sushi," or "Pine Sushi," which came from the prestigious restaurant at Atake. *Nigiri* sushi emerged during the Bunsei era (1818-30) and was originally served with the fish pre-seasoned.

寿司

歌川国芳「縞揃女弁慶　安宅の松」
大判錦絵　天保15年（1844）東京都立中央図書館所蔵
皿にのせた握り寿司を幼子がねだっています。歌舞伎の「安宅の松」という場面のパロディーで、娘が持つ寿司折箱のラベルが、安宅の高級店「松の寿司」となっているのがユーモラスです。文政期（1818-30）に始まった握り寿司は、当初ネタに味がついていました。

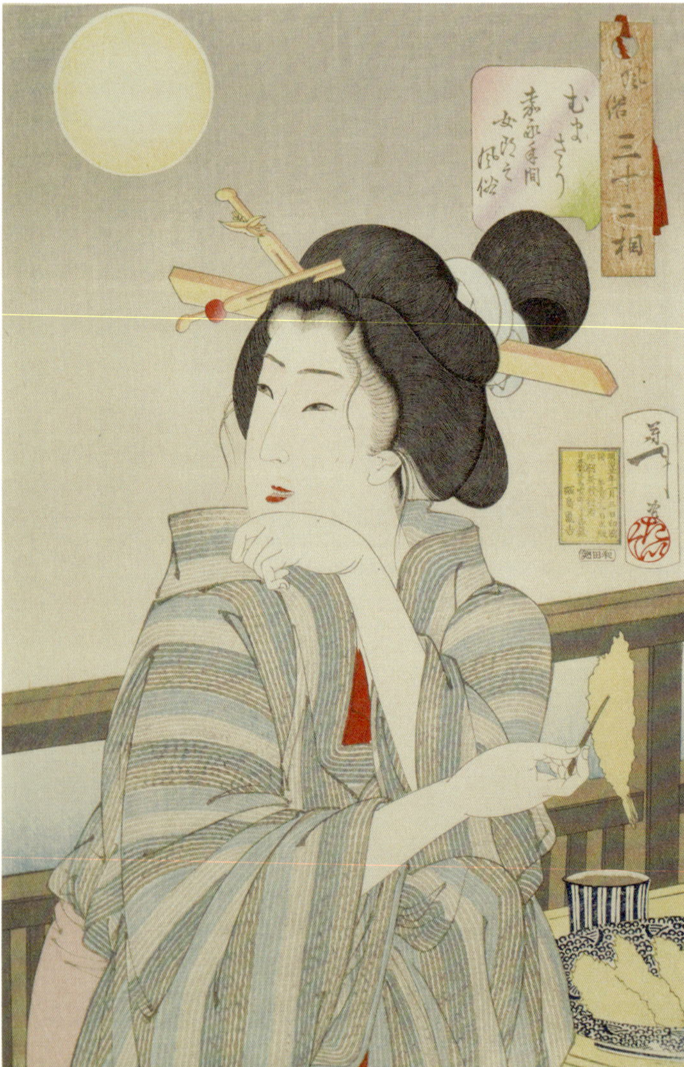
風俗三十二相

Tempura

Tsukioka Yoshitoshi, *Tasty,*
Appearance of a Prostitute in the Kaei era,
from the series *Thirty-two Aspects of Manners and Customs,*
1888, *oban nishiki-e*. Chiba City Museum of Art.

The *Thirty-two Aspects* series, originally referring to the Buddha's thirty-two auspicious aspects, creatively likens these to women of different eras. In this work, a woman from the Kaei era (1848-54) holds a skewer of fish tempura, with a soy sauce-based dipping sauce beside her.

天ぷら

月岡芳年「風俗三十二相 むまさう 嘉永年間女郎之風俗」
大判錦絵　明治21年（1888）　千葉市美術館所蔵

「三十二相」とは、本来仏様の32の優れた特徴を意味しています。これを時代ごとの女性の様相になぞらえて「〜そう」と題したシリーズです。この「むまさう（旨そう）」は、嘉永期（1848-54）に想定された女性が、魚の天ぷらを串で刺して持つ姿で、醤油を使った天つゆも用意されています。

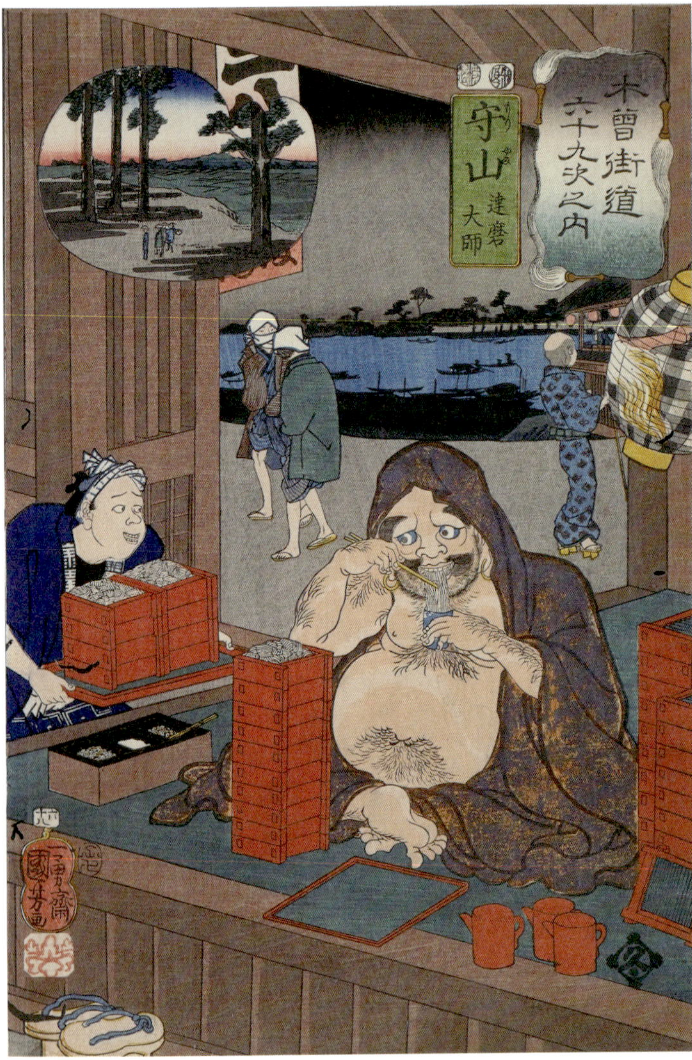
木曾街道六十九次之内
守山
達磨大師
一勇斎國芳画

Soba

Utagawa Kuniyoshi, *Moriyama: Daruma Taishi*, from the series *Sixty-nine Stations of the Kisokaido*,
1852, *oban nishiki-e*. Gifu Prefectural Museum.

The legendary monk Daruma heartily enjoys tray after tray of soba noodles. The Kisokaido road's Moriyama station puns on the common dish of *mori* soba noodles. Historically, soba (buckwheat) was eaten in a mochi-like form called *sobagaki*, but during the Edo period soba noodles gained popularity. By the late Edo period, soy sauce had become an essential seasoning for soba dipping sauce, which was served in a small bowl as held by Daruma in this print.

蕎麦

歌川国芳「木曽街道六十九次之内　守山　達磨大師」
大判錦絵　嘉永5年（1852）　岐阜県博物館所蔵
達磨大師が、豪快に蕎麦を食べ続けています。木曽街道の宿場「守山」は「盛り蕎麦」を連想させたのでしょう。古来蕎麦といえば餅状にして食べる蕎麦がきが通常でしたが、このような蕎麦切りが普及したのは、江戸時代のことでした。さらに幕末に普及した醤油が、麺つゆに欠かせない調味料となりました。

Famous Restaurants

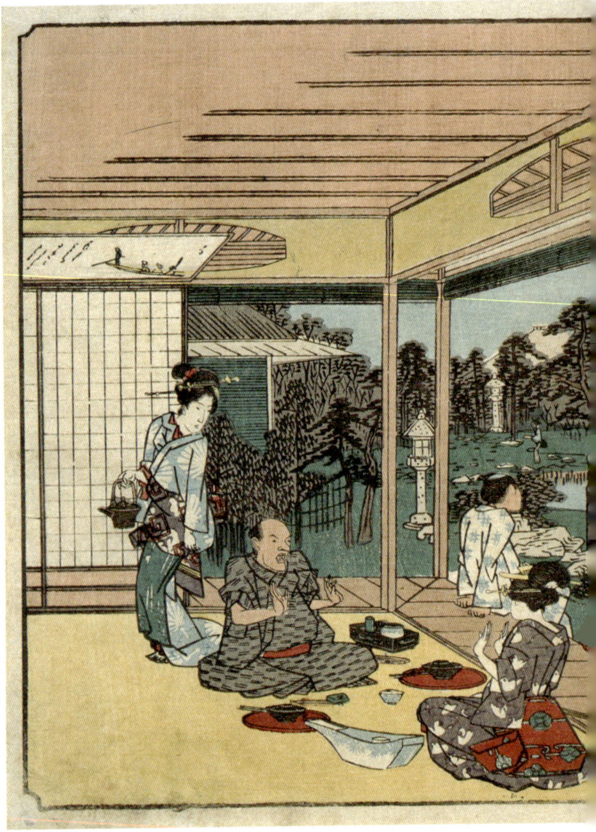

Utagawa Hiroshige, *Ushijima: Musashiya Restaurant*, from the series *Famous Restaurants of Edo*,
ca. 1835-44, *oban nishiki-e*. National Museum of Japanese History.

At the upscale Musashiya restaurant in Ushijima, owned by Musashiya Gonzaburo, a client and geisha play a *ken* hand game while a maid brings dishes on a large platter. In Japan, where individual trays were customary, the fashionable Chinese practice of serving food from a large platter to smaller dishes was a hallmark of high-class dining.

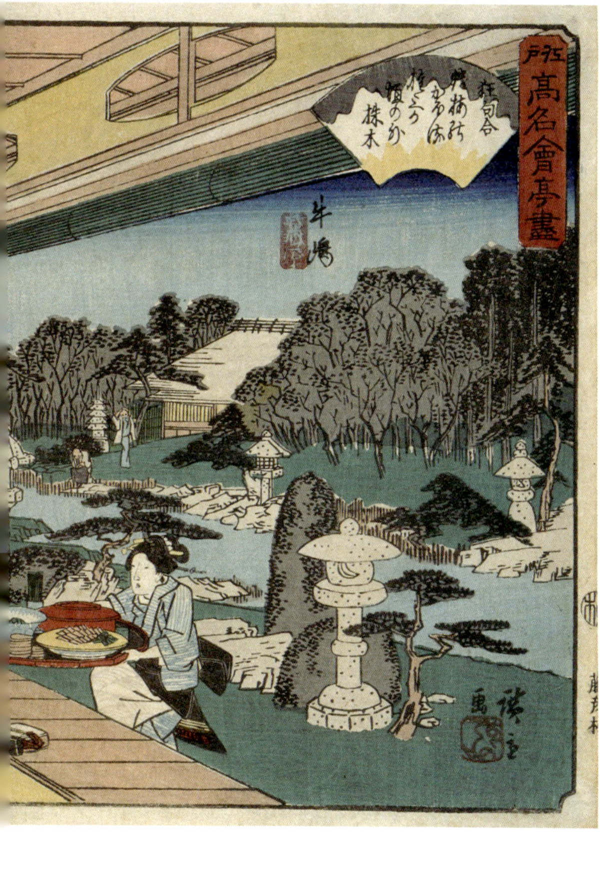

料亭

歌川広重「江戸高名会亭尽　牛嶋　武蔵屋」

大判錦絵　天保後期（1835-44）　国立歴史民俗博物館所蔵

牛島にあった高級料理店・武蔵屋（武蔵屋権三郎）で、客と芸妓が拳遊びをしているところに、仲居が大皿に盛った料理を運んできた場面です。銘々膳が基本であった日本で、大皿から料理を小皿に取り分けるのは、高級店で行われた中国スタイルのお洒落な食べ方でした。

Street Stalls

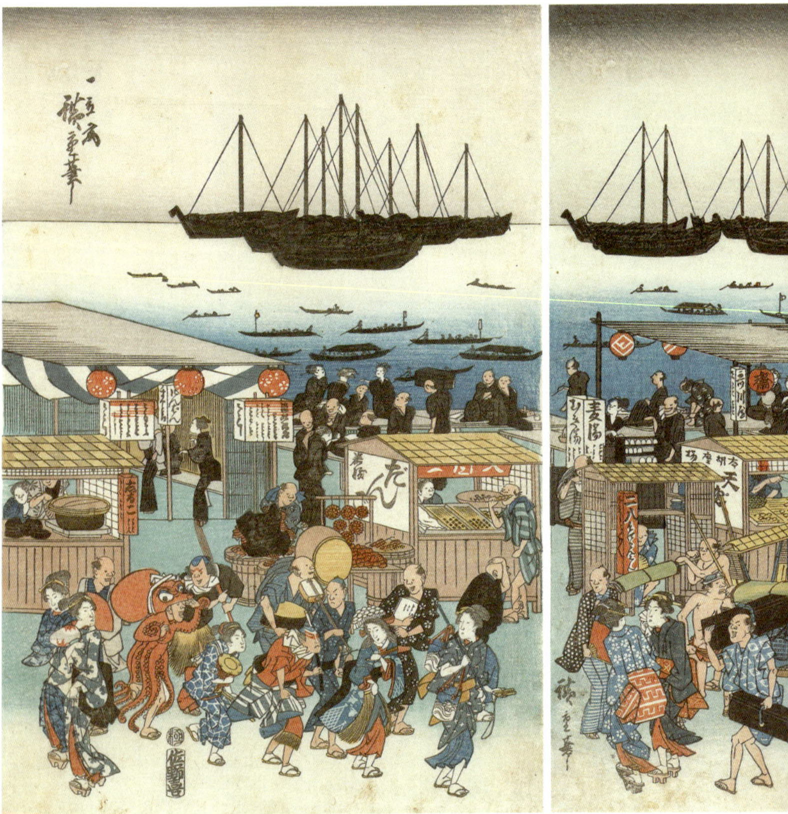

Utagawa Hiroshige, *Amusements While Waiting for the Moon on the Twenty-sixth Night at Takanawa*,
from the series *Famous Views of the Eastern Capital*,
1832-34, *oban nishiki-e* triptych. Hagi Uragami Museum.

Crowds gather on the coast to admire the moonlight during the *Nijurokuya Machi* (Twenty-sixth Night Wait) festival. Among the street stalls, vendors sell *nigiri* sushi. Unlike pre-seasoned sushi at high-end restaurants, at stalls customers adjusted flavor themselves using soy sauce provided in small bowls.

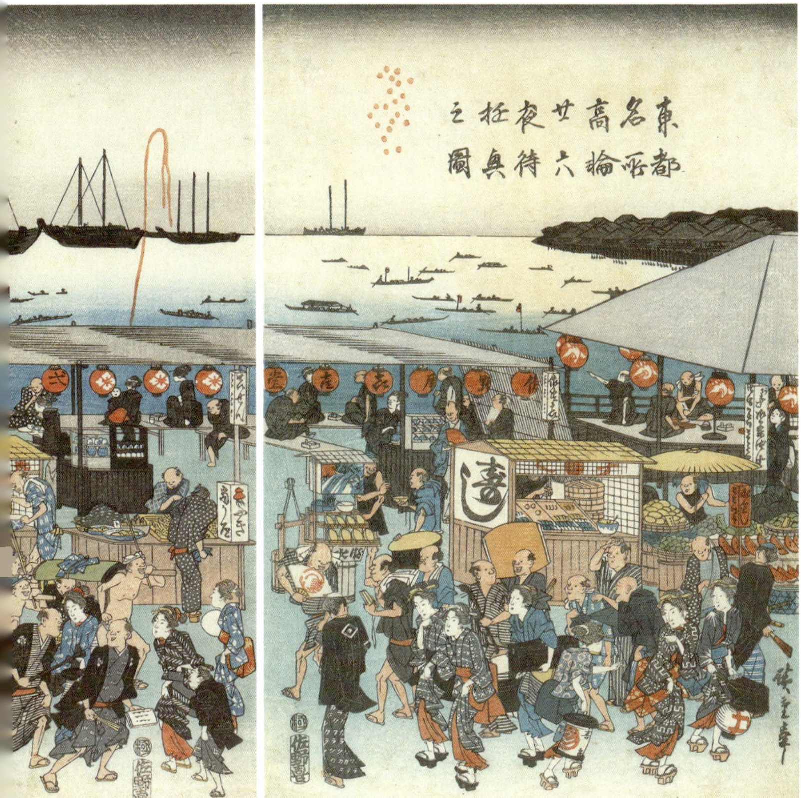

屋台

歌川広重「東都名所　高輪廿六夜待遊興之図」

大判錦絵３枚続　天保3-5年（1832-34）

山口県立萩美術館・浦上記念館所蔵

「二十六夜待」の夜は、月光を拝むため海岸に大勢の人々が集まりました。多くの屋台の中に握り寿司を出す店も見えます。高級料理店では、ネタに味がついていましたが、屋台では、鉢に醤油が入っていて、客が自分で味をつけるようになっていた様子がわかります。

Fish Market

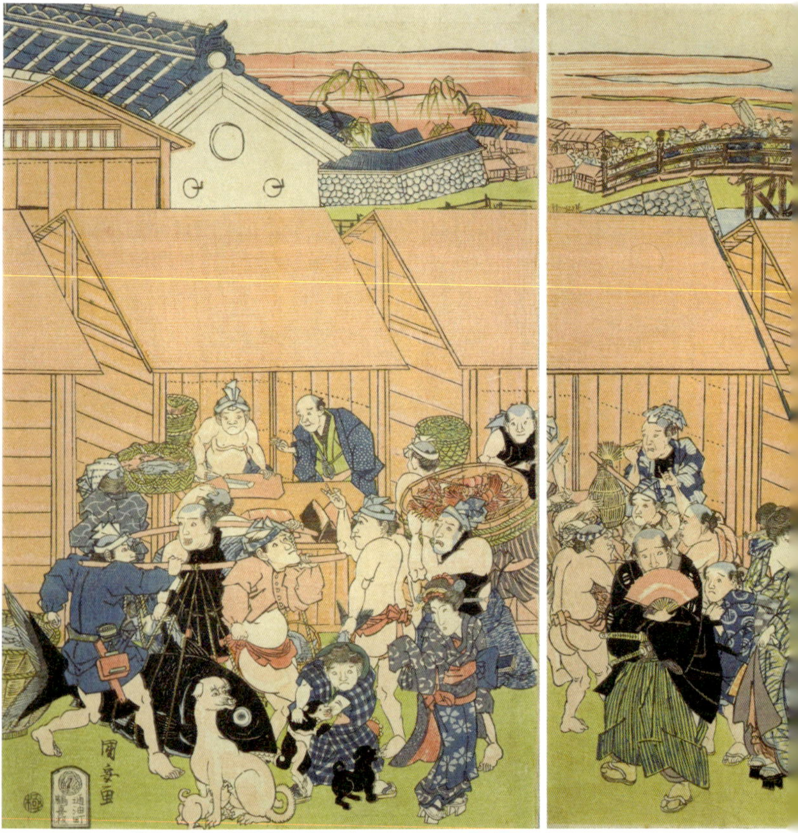

Utagawa Kuniyasu, *Prosperity of the Fish Market at Nihonbashi*, ca. 1830-32, *oban nishiki-e* triptych. National Diet Library.

The fish market at Nihonbashi, known as the "Kitchen of Edo," bustles with people in this vibrant scene, with various seafood meticulously illustrated. Fresh seafood was delivered to Nihonbashi in fast boats from Boshu (present-day Chiba prefecture).

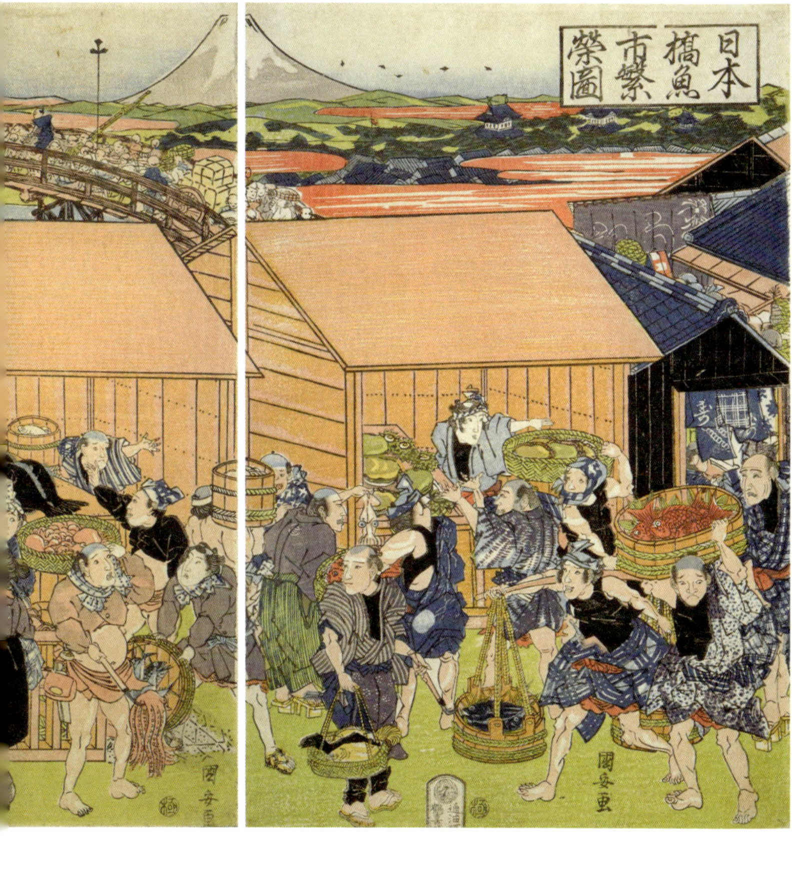

魚市場

歌川国安「日本橋魚市繁栄図」

大判錦絵3枚続　天保1-3年（1830-32）頃
国立国会図書館所蔵

「江戸の台所」と称される日本橋の魚河岸は、大勢の人々が行き交う活気ある様子で、さまざまな魚介類が詳細に描かれています。房州（現在の千葉県）からも速い船で、新鮮な海産物が日本橋に届けられました。

Chapter 5

Kabuki

第五章

歌舞伎

Popular Entertainment

Kabuki, a quintessential Japanese performing art, originated in the early Edo period and soon became the foremost popular entertainment. Early forms such as *onna kabuki* by women and *wakashu kabuki* by young boys were banned for their provocative nature. In their place came *yaro kabuki*, performed by adult men—a tradition that persists today, with male actors known as *onnagata* portraying female roles.

Since their emergence in the 1680s, kabuki prints have been as significant in ukiyo-e as *bijinga*. Indeed, artists of the Torii school, founded by Torii Kiyonobu (1664-1729) upon moving from Osaka to Edo in 1687 with his father, an *onnagata* actor, can be credited with broadly popularizing ukiyo-e through their single-sheet prints featuring individual actors. From Kiyonobu's time to this day, the Torii school has created signboards for kabuki theaters as well as producing a vast number of *yakusha-e* (actor prints), continually matching the evolving repertoire of kabuki plays to attract numerous buyers. These prints soared in popularity during a play's run, particularly *hosoban* (p. 107) prints known for their small size and accessibility.

大衆の娯楽

歌舞伎は江戸時代初期に始まった日本を代表する芸能であり、長く人々の最大の娯楽となりました。当初行われた女性が演じる女歌舞伎や、若い男性が演じる若衆歌舞伎は、風紀を乱す演出として禁じられ、成人男性が主演する野郎歌舞伎が行われるようになりましたが、この伝統は現代にも続いており、女役も男性が演じています。

浮世絵においては、その発祥当初の1680年代から、歌舞伎絵は美人画と並んで重要な主題でしたが、個々の役者を一枚摺の版画に取り上げ、ひいては浮世絵版画の普及にも貢献したのは、鳥居派の絵師たちであったといえるでしょう。貞享4年(1687)に、大坂の女形役者であったという父とともに江戸に下ったと伝えられる鳥居清信(1664-1729)を初代として、鳥居派は現代に至るまで芝居小屋の絵看板制

Around 1768, Katsukawa Shunsho (1743-92) changed the course of actor prints. He began to faithfully depict actors' true likenesses, redefining a genre that had previously paid little attention to actual appearance. With Shunsho's breakthrough, realistic portraits became the standard, fulfilling a role much like that of collectible photographs for devoted fans.

作を家業としていました。一方で、鳥居派によって膨大な役者絵が版画で出版されており、その速報性が演目の入れ替わりの早い歌舞伎の世界にも合致して、多くの人々がこれを買い求めた状況が想像できます。ただし芝居に取材した役者絵は、その芝居が上演されている期間が売り時であり、特に細判（p.107）と呼ばれる小さな画面の作品は、安い消耗品的な商品であったと思われます。

役者絵の方向性を変えたのは、勝川春章（1743-92）でした。明和5年（1768）頃から役者を似顔で描くことを本格的に始め、それまでほとんど実際の容貌を描く意識を持たなかった役者絵を一新します。そして以降は、役者絵であれば当然のように似顔で描かれることが求められ、特定の役者を贔屓するファンにとっては、ブロマイドのような役割を果たしました。

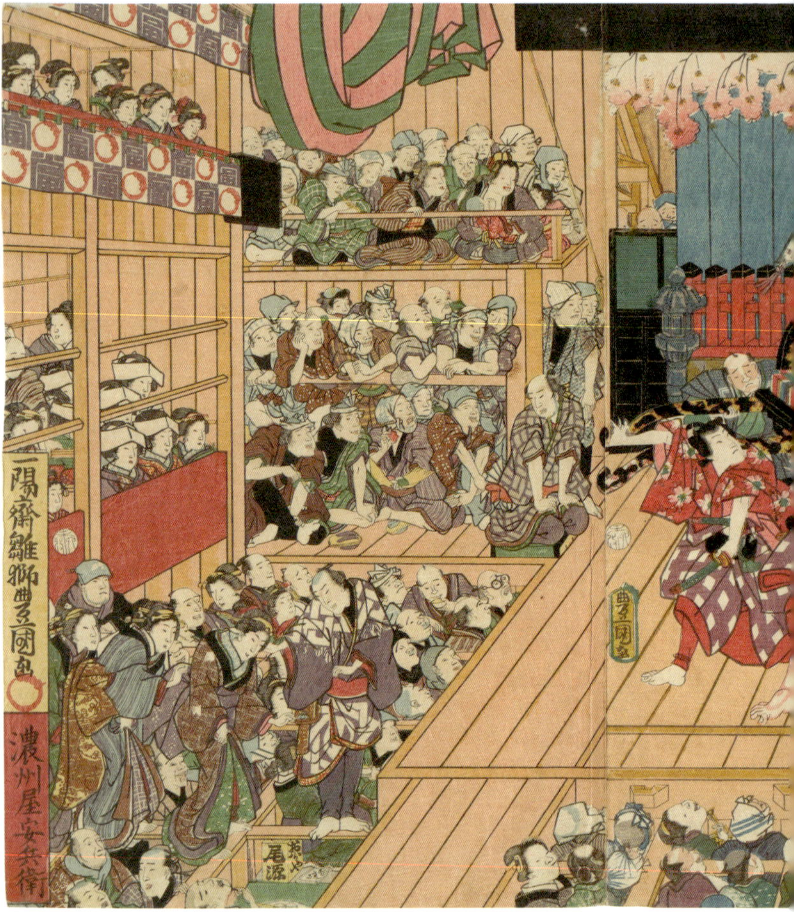

Utagawa Toyokuni III,
Flourishing Business at a Major Theater,
1859, *oban nishiki-e* triptych. Tokyo Metropolitan Library.

Inside a theater, audience members behave as they please while enjoying a dynamic stage performance. In the high-grade box seats along the left wall, samurai-class female attendants in *ageboshi* (headscarves) sit watching in orderly fashion.

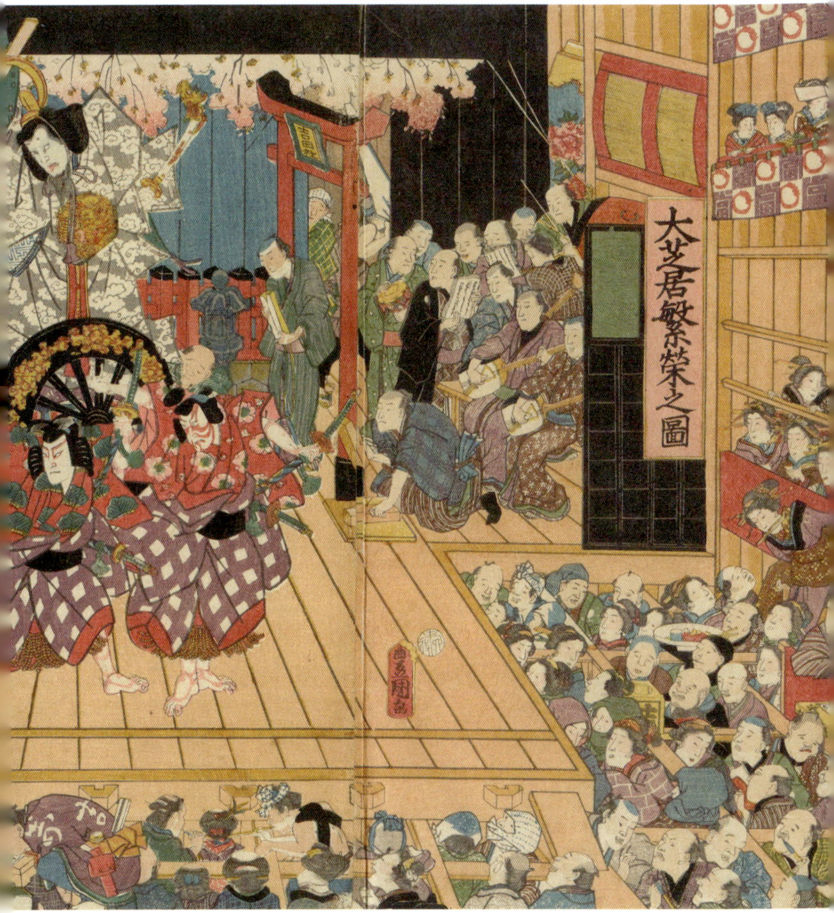

三代歌川豊国「大芝居繁栄之図」

大判錦絵3枚続　安政6年（1859）　東京都立中央図書館所蔵

芝居小屋の内部を描いた作品で、人々が思い思いの姿で迫力ある舞台を楽しんでいます。左壁沿いの桟敷席は上等席で、揚げ帽子をかぶった奥女中が整然と座って観劇する様子も描かれています。

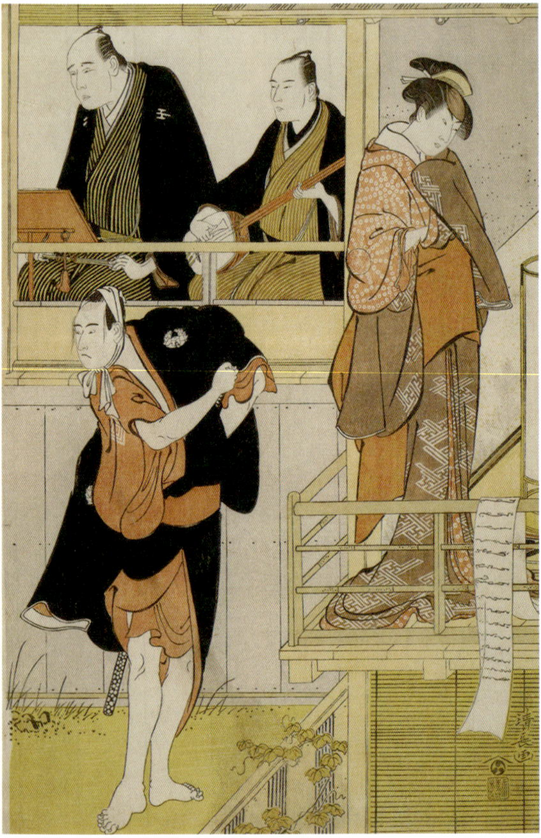

Torii Kiyonaga, *The Actors Ichikawa Yaozo III as Furuteya Hachirobei and Nakamura Riko as Tanbaya Otsuma,*

1785, *oban nishiki-e*. Chiba City Museum of Art.

Kiyonaga, artist of the Torii school, imbued his works with realism through the inclusion of not only the actors on stage, but also the *shamisen* (three-stringed Japanese lute) player and *joruri* (p. 108) narrator, known as the *tayu*.

鳥居清長「三代目市川八百蔵の古手屋八郎兵衛と中村里好の丹波屋おつま」

大判錦絵　天明5年（1785）　千葉市美術館所蔵

鳥居派の清長は、舞台で演技をする役者とともに、三味線と浄瑠璃（p.108）の語り手である太夫という出語り連中の姿も描き込んで、作品に臨場感を加えています。

Katsukawa Shunko,
The Actor Ichikawa Danjuro V
ca. 1789-90, *oban nishiki-e*. Keio University.

Ichikawa Danjuro (p. 108) was Edo's most celebrated actor, brought to life in this portrait. The grand and striking depiction of his face gives the impression that he is within arm's reach, similar to a prized fan photograph.

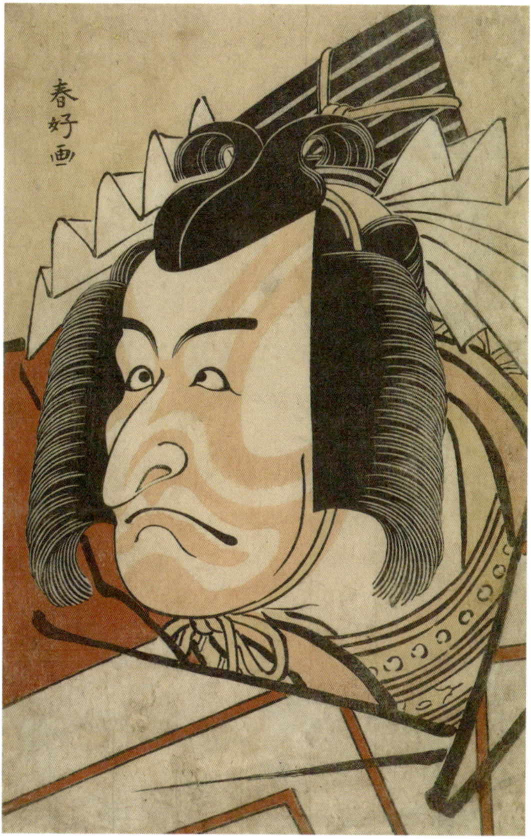

勝川春好「五代目市川團十郎」
大判錦絵　天明9年 - 寛政2年 (1789-90)　慶應義塾所蔵
市川團十郎 (p.108) は、江戸で一番の人気役者の名跡。画面に大きく顔を描き、眼前に役者を見るような迫力ある似顔絵は、ファンにとって現代のブロマイドのようなものでした。

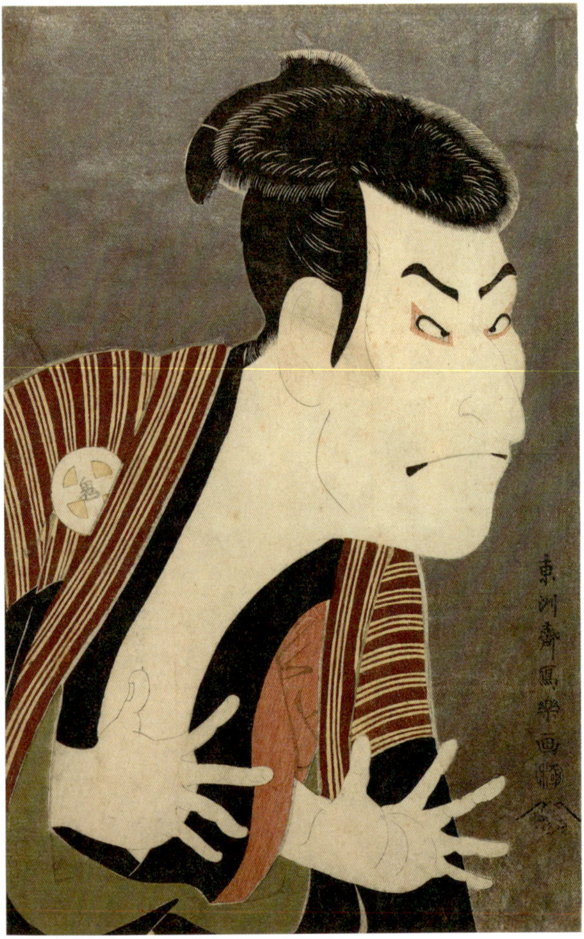

Toshusai Sharaku, *The Actor Otani Oniji III as Edobei* and *Ichikawa Omezo as Yakko Ippei*,
1794, *oban nishiki-e*. Tokyo National Museum.

A print pair portraying a kabuki scene where the villainous Edobei lunges at the character Ippei in an attempt to steal public money. Sharaku's tendency to emphasize the imperfections in actors' faces reportedly did not garner favor among fans of his day.

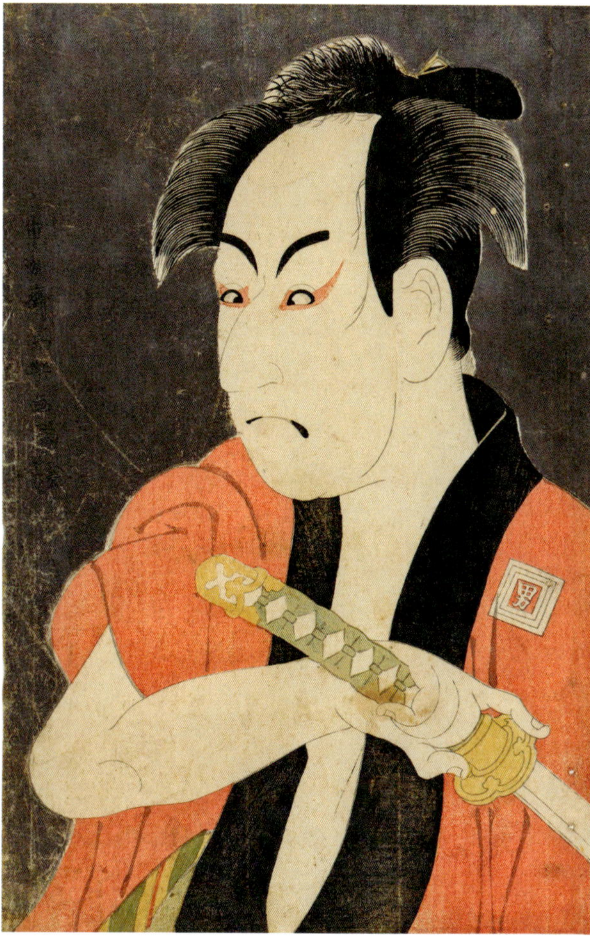

東洲斎写楽「三代目大谷鬼次の江戸兵衛」〈左ページ〉
「市川男女蔵の奴一平」

大判錦絵　寛政6年（1794）　東京国立博物館所蔵

悪役の江戸兵衛が奴一平を襲い、公金を奪うシーンが題材となった2枚組です。写楽は、役者の顔の欠点までも強調して描いてしまうため、当時の役者ファンの人気は得られなかったと伝えられています。

ColBase（https://colbase.nich.go.jp/）

Chapter 6

Yoshiwara

第六章

吉原

Yoshiwara Sophistication

Yoshiwara, Edo's only licensed pleasure district, flourished under the shogunate's auspices, captivating the imaginations of many. Among the more than 2,000 courtesans residing within its confines, ukiyo-e works primarily showcased elite courtesans (*oiran* p. 109). These *oiran*, unattainable to the average person, were highly educated, skilled in various arts, and revered as the epitome of beauty and grace. In Yoshiwara's self-regulated society, a tapestry of singular customs, even a samurai's status could not automatically command favor. Instead, the most esteemed clients were cultured, affluent connoisseurs, able to wield their intellect as deftly as their swords and appreciate the nuances of art with subtlety and grace. Yoshiwara geisha, who held their craft in the highest of regard, were strictly prohibited from the sale of sexual services.

吉原の粋(いき)

江戸で唯一の幕府公認の遊廓として栄えたのが吉原でした。浮世絵に主に描かれたのは、閉ざされた遊廓で2000人以上いたという遊女の中でも一握りの高位の遊女（花魁(おいらん) p.109）で、決して一般庶民が相手にできる存在ではありませんでした。諸芸に通じ高い教養を身につけた理想的な美しい女性として、花魁は崇められる対象でもありました。独特の習慣と自治権を持った吉原遊廓では、武士だからといって遊女にもてるわけではありません。武士であっても刀を置き、文化芸術など物事に通じ、それをひけらかすことなく、同時に金払いのよい粋な通人(つうじん)が最上の客とされました。また吉原芸者は、最高の芸を売る芸能者としての誇りを持ち、性を売ることは厳しく禁

Beyond the officially sanctioned Yoshiwara, lesser-known pleasure quarters, including the Nihonbashi area, Fukagawa, and Mukojima thrived in the vicinity of the Sumida River. While Yoshiwara geisha were unmistakably distinct from ordinary women, those of unlicensed districts exhibited a rich diversity in appearance, with each district's cultural nuances vividly depicted in prints of the time. But as unskilled women were increasingly drawn into the world of casual geisha and illicit prostitution, the shogunate intervened.

じられていました。

官許の吉原以外の遊里、すなわち日本橋界隈や深川、向島など隅田川周辺の歓楽街も町人には人気でした。吉原のように一般女性の姿との違いが明確ではありませんが、浮世絵は、それぞれの場所ごとに風俗的な特徴があったことを示しています。ただし芸もないのに気軽に芸者になり、同時に性を売る私娼もいたため、幕府による取り締まりの対象ともなりました。

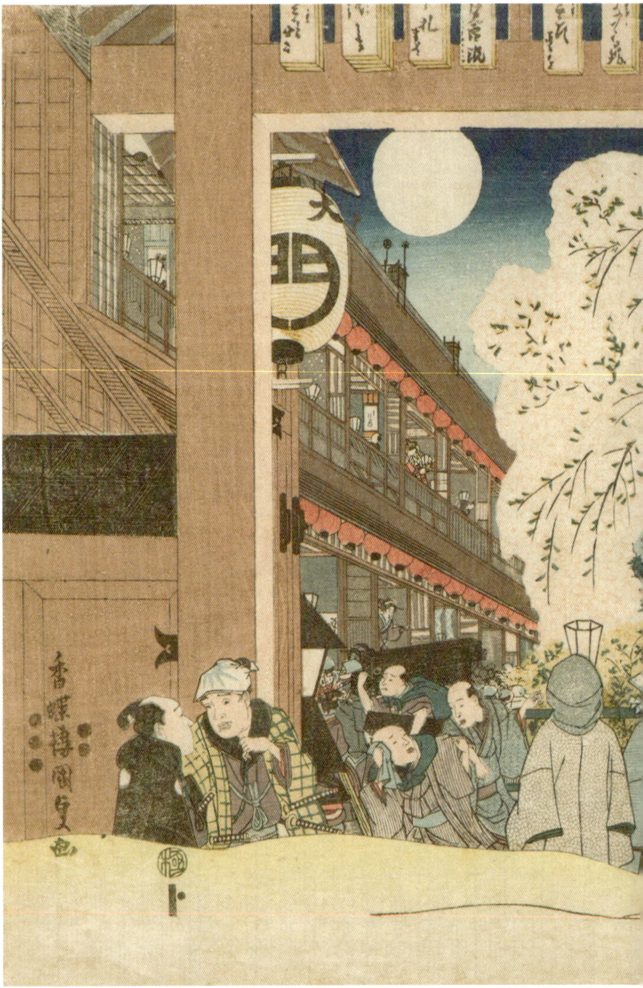

Utagawa Kunisada, *Cherry Blossoms in the Moonlight in the Yoshiwara Pleasure District*,
ca. 1833, *oban nishiki-e*. Kanagawa Prefectural Museum of Cultural History.

Yoshiwara's main gate, the sole entrance to the pleasure district, looms large in the foreground, framing cherry blossoms in full bloom. Each year, cherry trees were planted along Yoshiwara's main street, creating a lavish 250-meter stretch of blossom during flowering season.

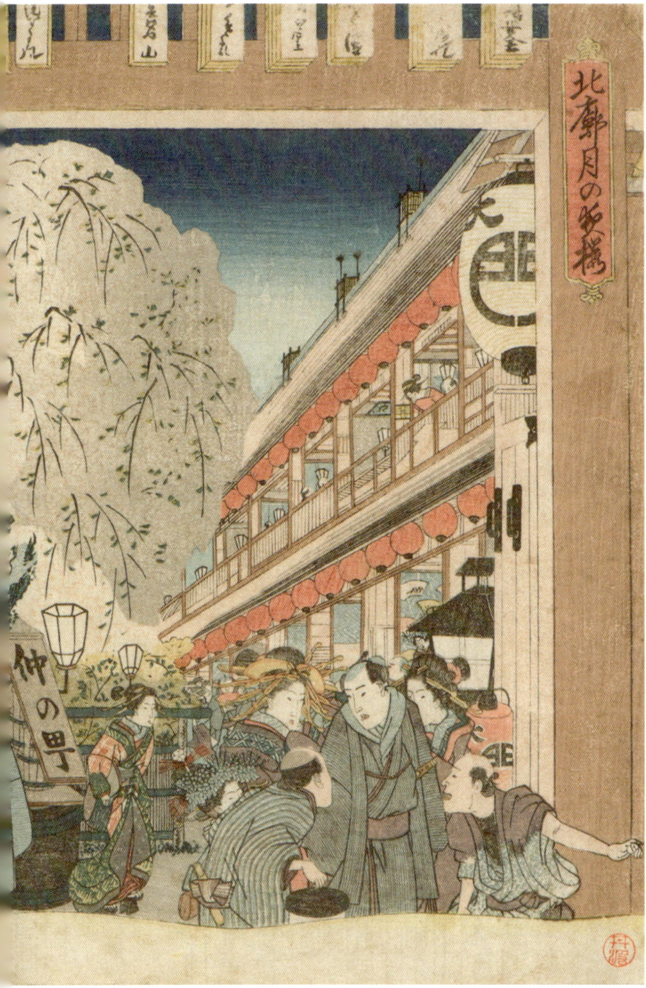

歌川国貞「北廓月の夜桜」

大判錦絵　天保4年（1833）頃　神奈川県立歴史博物館所蔵

吉原遊廓唯一の出入口である大門を、手前に額縁のように大きく描き、満開の桜を正面に見ています。吉原の桜樹は、毎年花が咲く季節にその都度メインストリートに約250mにわたって植えられたという、豪気なものでした。

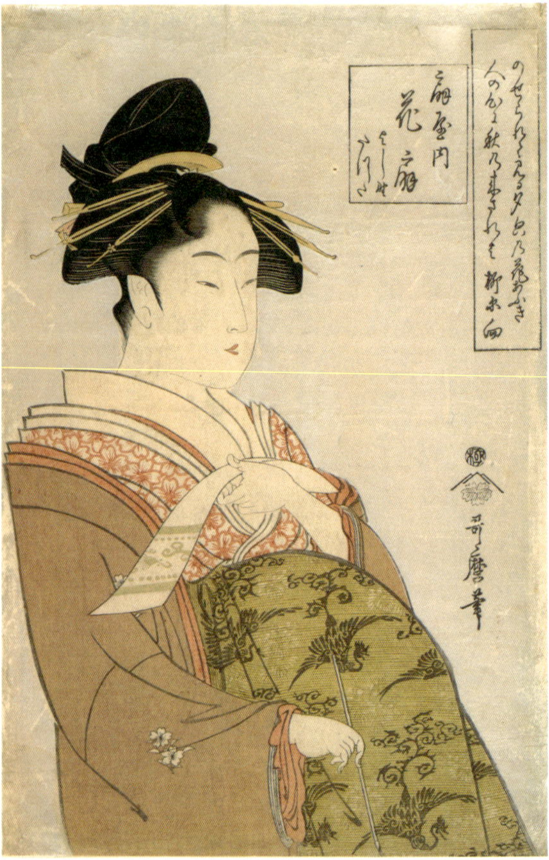

Kitagawa Utamaro, *The Oiran Hanaogi of Ogiya*,
ca. 1793-94, *oban nishiki-e*. Metropolitan Museum of Art.

In the elite Yoshiwara brothel Ogiya, the eminent courtesan Hanaogi holds a *tanzaku* (poem card) and brush, preparing to compose a verse—a symbol of her refined intellect.

喜多川歌麿「扇屋内　花扇」
大判錦絵　寛政5-6年（1793-94）頃　メトロポリタン美術館所蔵
吉原遊廓の中でも格式の高い妓楼・扇屋。その筆頭遊女の名跡が花扇です。短冊と筆を手に歌を詠もうとする姿に、教養の高さを感じさせます。

Keisai Eisen, *Daikoku Dance on New Year's Day: Koimurasaki of Tamaya*, from the series *Four Seasons in the Pleasure Quarters: Annual Events in the Yoshiwara*, ca. 1823, *oban nishiki-e*. Chiba City Museum of Art.

A courtesan wears an opulent *uchikake* (formal outer kimono) featuring wave and dragon motifs, her hair embellished with ornate *kushi kanzashi* (decorative hair combs), in a striking representation of the pinnacle of Yoshiwara's refined aesthetic.

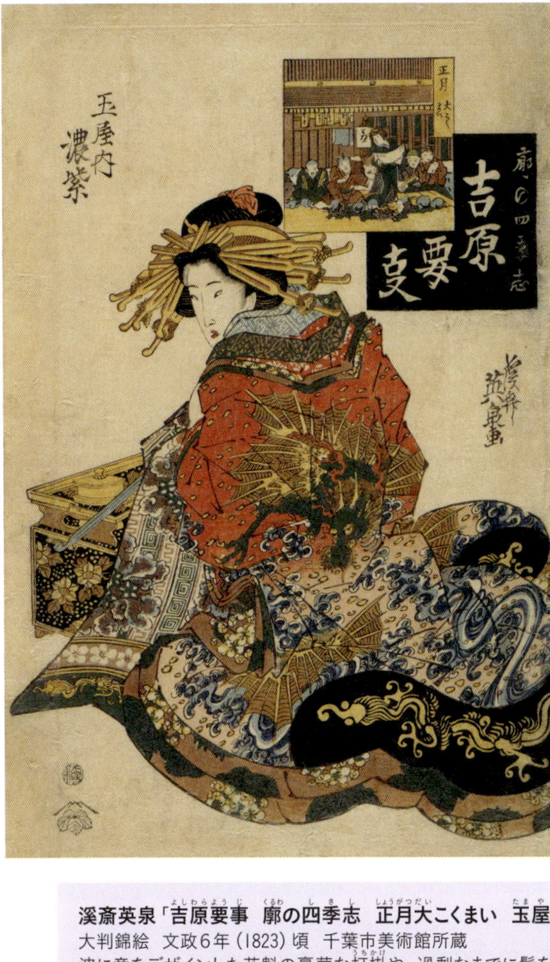

渓斎英泉「吉原要事　廓の四季志　正月大こくまい　玉屋内濃紫」
大判錦絵　文政6年（1823）頃　千葉市美術館所蔵
波に竜をデザインした花魁の豪華な打掛や、過剰なまでに髪を飾る櫛簪に目を奪われます。吉原の美意識もここに極まれりといったところです。

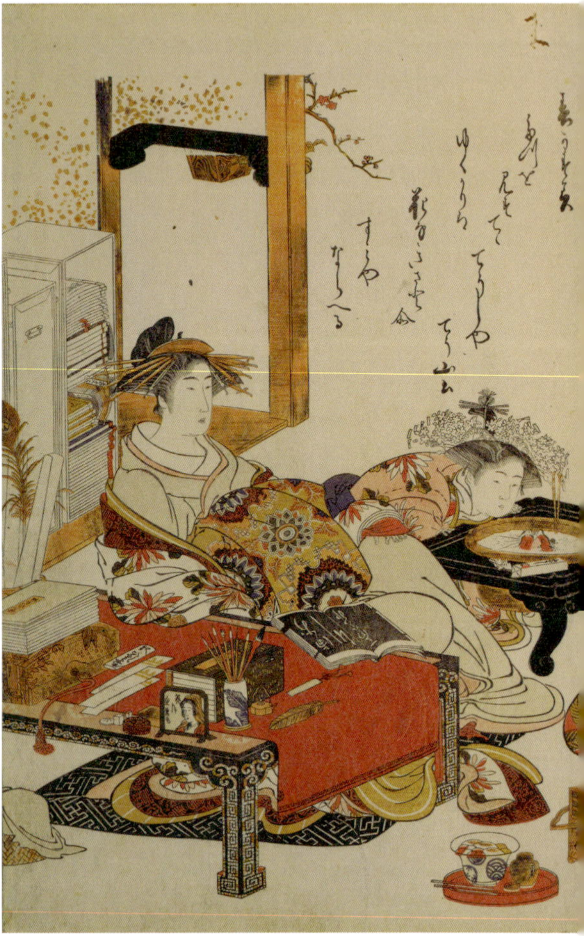

Kitao Masanobu, *The Handwriting of Modern Beauties in Yoshiwara*,
1784, color print illustration from accordion-fold book.
Chiba City Museum of Art.

Hinazuru and Chozan, illustrious courtesans of the elite Chojiya brothel, were acclaimed for their calligraphy. Accompanied by their actual handwriting, this print depicts the courtesans in splendid attire, surrounded by *shinzo* (apprentice courtesans) and *kamuro* (young attendants).

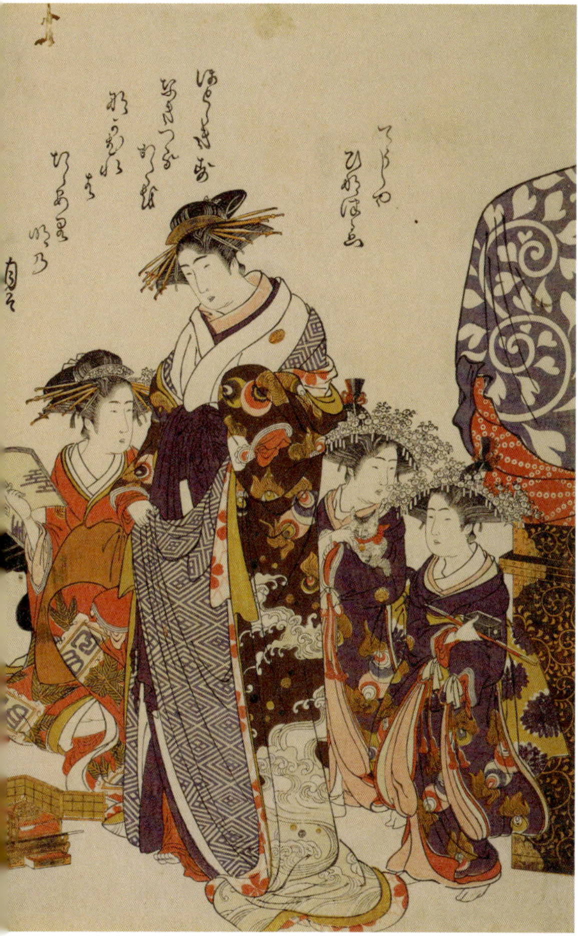

北尾政演「吉原傾城新美人合自筆鏡」

彩色摺画帖　1帖　天明4年（1784）　千葉市美術館所蔵

丁字屋の名跡ひな鶴と丁山は、書の名手としても知られていました。その筆跡をそのまま版にして、豪華な衣装を着た2人を新造や禿たちとともに描き出した図です。

Chapter 7

Cats

第七章

猫

Affection for Cats and Playful Humor

In Japan, the term *neko kawaigari* (lit. cat affection) refers to excessive pampering and fondness, akin to the adoration one might show a pet cat. By the Heian period (794-1185), cats had already become beloved companions in Japanese households. In ukiyo-e, cats were depicted far more frequently than dogs, despite both being common pets.

Their overwhelming presence can be largely attributed to the famous artist Utagawa Kuniyoshi (1797-1861). Kuniyoshi's love for cats is well-known; he kept cats himself and observed them with a great fondness evident in his many works. Whether depicting everyday life with cats, anthropomorphized cats, or playful feline puns, his works are rich with humor and a delight for fellow cat lovers. When the Tempo Reforms of 1842 banned depictions of kabuki actors, Kuniyoshi defied the restrictions by creating works that humorously featured cats with faces resembling actors, showcasing his rebellious spirit and further endearing him to the public.

猫好きとユーモア

日本には「猫可愛がり」という言葉があります。猫を可愛がるように、むやみに甘やかして可愛がることをいいますが、少なくとも平安時代（794-1185）には、猫は愛玩動物として、人間とともに暮らすようになっていたようです。浮世絵にもさまざまな場面で猫が描かれてきており、同じ愛玩動物の犬よりはるかに多く作品が知られています。

猫が描かれる浮世絵が膨大に出版された最大の要因をつくったのは、浮世絵師の中でも特に猫好きとして知られる歌川国芳（1797-1861）でした。この絵師の猫好きは有名で、自らも猫を飼い、愛情を持ってその生態を観察していたであろうことは、その多くの作品によって知ることができます。室内の光景に猫が現れるような風俗図はもちろん、猫を擬人化したり、駄洒落と組み合わせたり、いずれの作品もユーモアにあふれ、猫好きの鑑賞者にはたまらない作品群でした。天保の改革により、天保13年（1842）に歌舞伎役者を描くことが禁じられた時代には、猫の顔を役者の似顔にした作品を出版して反骨精神をあらわにし、国芳は町人たちから一層の支持を得ています。

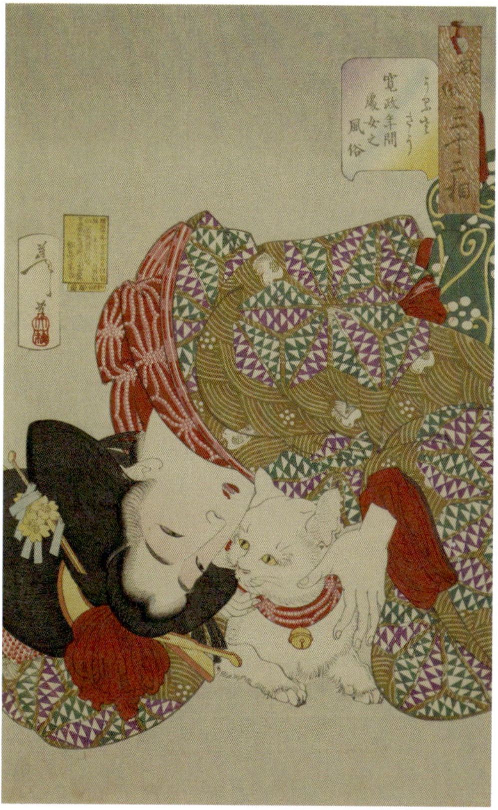

Tsukioka Yoshitoshi, *Tiresome, Mannerisms of a Girl from the Kansei era*, from the series *Thirty-two Aspects and Customs*,
1888, *oban nishiki-e*. Chiba City Museum of Art.

A young girl affectionately strokes the neck of a cat, embracing it closely. The title implies that the cat is somewhat bothered by the girl's excessive affection.

月岡芳年「風俗三十二相　うるささう　寛政年間處女之風俗」
大判錦絵　明治21年（1888）　千葉市美術館所蔵
若い娘が抱きつくようにして、猫の喉を撫でています。題名からすると、娘の愛情余って猫は少し迷惑そうにしているという様子なのでしょう。

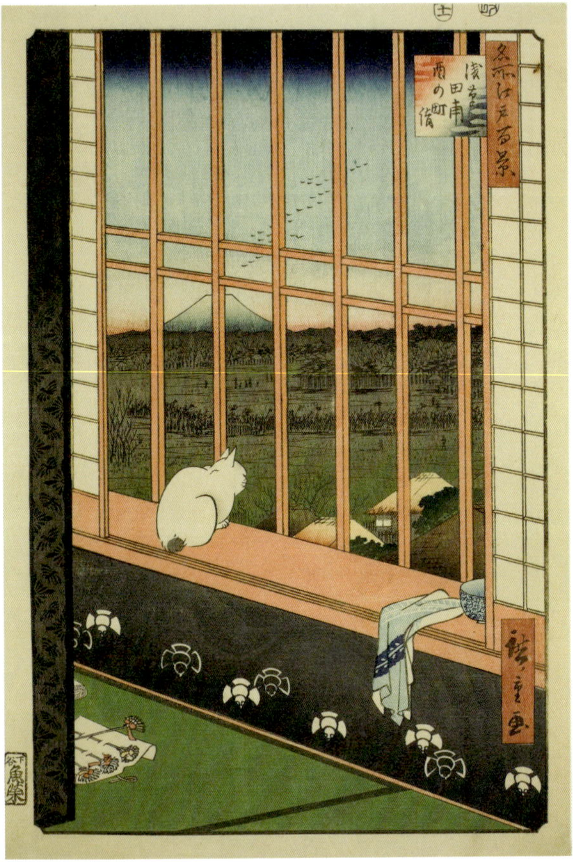

Utagawa Hiroshige, *Asakusa Rice Fields and Torinomachi Festival*, from the series *One Hundred Famous Views of Edo*,
1857, *oban nishiki-e*. The Art Institute of Chicago.

A cat gazes out from a Yoshiwara courtesan's second-floor room. Mount Fuji stands in the distance, while a procession bearing *kumade* (bamboo rakes) returns from the *Tori no Ichi* (Torinomachi festival).

歌川広重「名所江戸百景　浅草田圃酉の町詣」
大判錦絵　安政4年（1857）シカゴ美術館所蔵
吉原遊廓の2階、遊女の部屋から1匹の猫が外を眺めています。遠景に富士山、中景の田圃には「酉の市」帰りの縁起物の熊手を手にした人々の列が見えます。

Utagawa Kuniyoshi, *Bonito*, from the series *Cat's Substitute Characters*, 1843, *oban nishiki-e*. Private collection.

Katsuo (bonito) was a favorite fish among the people of Edo and also a delicacy for cats. Here, cats and bonito are cleverly combined to form the characters for the Japanese word.

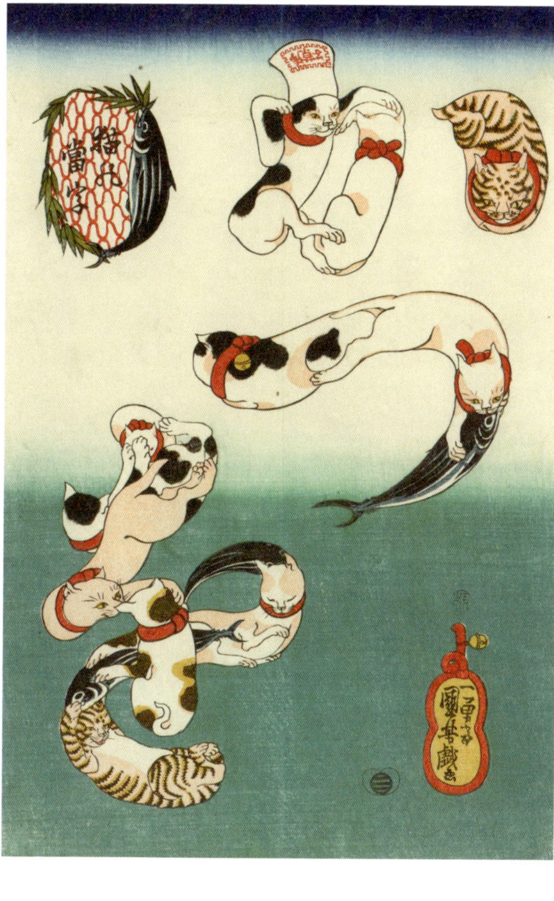

歌川国芳「猫の当字　かつを」

大判錦絵　天保14年(1843)　個人蔵

鰹は江戸の人々に好まれた魚ですが、猫の大好物でもあります。猫と鰹を組み合わせて、「かつを」という字を形作っています。

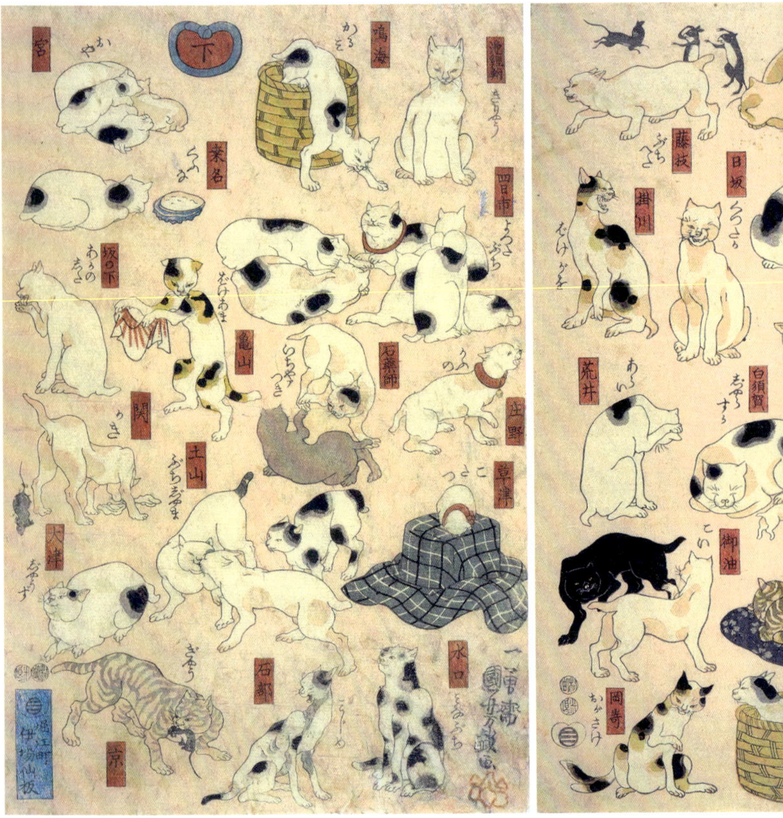

Utagawa Kuniyoshi, *Cats Suggested as the Fifty-three Stations of the Tokaido,*
1848, *oban nishiki-e* triptych. Gallery Beniya.

The 53 stations of the Tokaido road are whimsically depicted as cats in an array of poses. When it comes to cats, Kuniyoshi's skill is peerless.

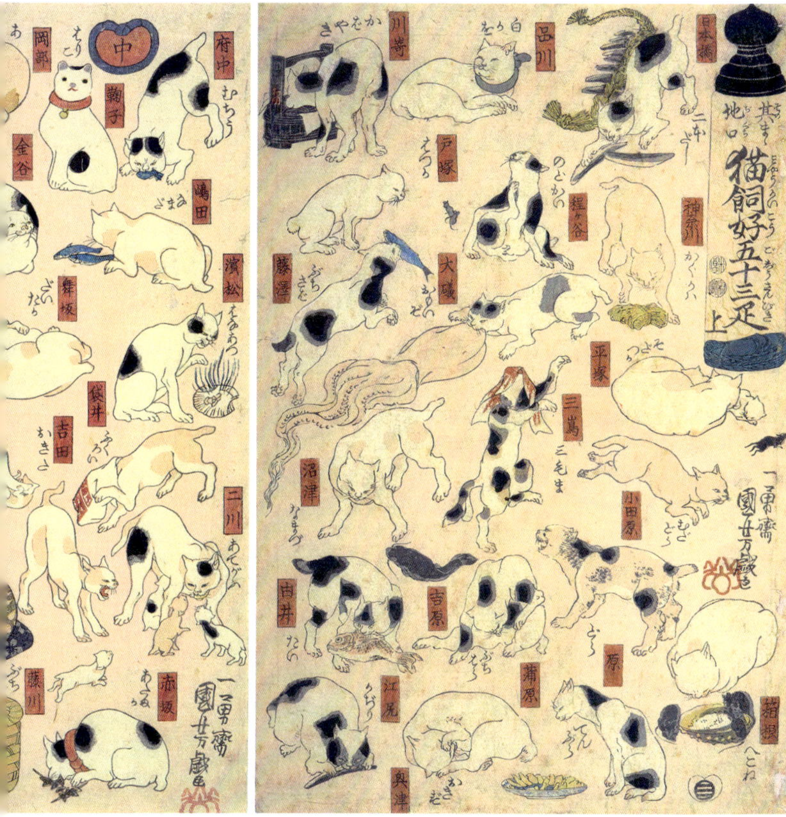

歌川国芳「其まゝ地口　猫飼好五十三疋　上中下」
大判錦絵３枚続　嘉永元年（1848）　ギャラリー紅屋
東海道五十三次の各宿場名を、猫たちの53の姿態になぞらえて洒落たユーモラスな作品です。猫を描かせたら国芳の右に出る絵師はいないでしょう。

Appendix

Glossary
Ukiyo-e Artists

付録

用語集
浮世絵師

Glossary | 用語集

Introduction

Yoshiwara Pleasure Quarters

The only pleasure quarters in Edo officially sanctioned by the shogunate. The establishment of the Yoshiwara district was likely motivated by concerns over the unchecked proliferation of brothels in the new capital. Initially, brothels were concentrated in Nihonbashi's Fukiya-cho district (present-day Ningyo-cho). Fear over public morals, however, due to their location in the bustling heart of Edo, led to their relocation to the remote outskirts behind Asakusa. The new quarters became known as *Shin Yoshiwara* (New Yoshiwara), while the original site was referred to as *Moto Yoshiwara* (Old Yoshiwara) to distinguish between the two.

はじめに

吉原遊廓

よしわらゆうかく

江戸で唯一の幕府公認の遊里。新しい首都となった江戸で、遊女屋が際限なく増えることへの懸念も吉原遊廓を開く理由であったと思われる。当初は日本橋葺屋町（現在の日本橋人形町）のあたりに遊女屋が集められたが、繁栄する江戸の中心地となったことによる風紀上の懸念から移転を迫られ、浅草の裏の辺鄙な場所へと移った。移転後の遊里を新吉原、移転前は元吉原と呼んで区別されている。

Chapter 1

dosa-biki

The process of treating ukiyo-e print paper with *dosa*, a solution of *nikawa* (animal glue) and *myoban* (alum). *Dosa*, applied with a brush to highly absorbent *washi* (Japanese paper), prevents pigment from seeping through and helps it adhere to the surface of the paper, improving color vibrancy. Additionally, it strengthens the paper, making it more durable to better withstand printing with a *baren*.

baren

A disc-shaped printing pad used to press the paper against the inked woodblock, aiding the transfer and permeation of ink from block to paper. The core of the pad consists of a flat coil of finely split bamboo cord. This is placed on a disc known as an *ategawa*, made of layers of paper coated with lacquer to harden them, and then wrapped in bamboo leaf, with the knot used as a handle. Today, only few craftsmen remain who can make *baren* using the traditional technique of finely splitting and weaving bamboo.

第一章

礬水引き どうさびき

膠と明礬を混ぜた溶液である礬水を、浮世絵版画の用紙に刷毛で引くことをいう。和紙はそのままだと浸透性が高すぎて、絵の具が紙の裏に抜けてしまう。礬水を引くことにより、摺った絵の具が紙表に定着し、発色も良くなる。さらに紙に強さも与えるため、バレンによる強い摺りにも耐えることができる。

バレン

浮世絵版画を摺る時に必要な道具。絵の具をつけた版木に紙を当ててバレンで摺ることで、絵の具が紙に浸透する。竹を細く裂いて編んだ紐を渦巻状にした芯に、重ねた紙に漆を塗って固めたものを当て（当皮）、これを竹皮で巻いて結び目を把手とする。現在では、竹を細く裂いて編み、伝統的な技術でバレンを作ることができる職人はわずかしかいない。

ookubi-e

A style of ukiyo-e print characterized by large, prominent portraits of faces, often including half-length and three-quarter-length figures. *Ookubi-e* were believed to have come about as a result of popular demand from fans of kabuki actors, with *ookubi-e* emerging in the *bijinga* (lit. pictures of beautiful women) genre shortly thereafter. In *bijinga*, even when depicting real courtesans, authentic likeness was not the primary focus; instead, artists aimed to express women's nature and social position through delicate gestures or subtle details in their kimono, thereby creating art that tested artists' true skill. *Ookubi-e* gained popularity after the Kansei era (1789-1801), but were temporarily banned in 1800 because they were considered to be overly conspicuous.

大首絵 おおくびえ

人物の顔を大きく捉えた構図の作品をこのように呼ぶ。半身像や七分身像も含まれる。役者ファンが顔を大きく描いた似顔絵を求めたことをきっかけに、大首絵が描かれるようになったと考えられるが、美人画における大首絵の発生は役者絵より少し遅れている。美人大首絵では、実在の遊女らを描く場合でも似顔の意識は薄く、着物の一部やわずかな仕草で女性の性質や立場を表現して魅力的な作品とする必要があるため、一層絵師の技量が試される。寛政期（1789-1801）以降盛んになるが、寛政12年（1800）に何かと目立つという理由で大首絵が禁止され、一時的に出版が控えられた時期があった。

Chapter 3

Gokaido

The five highways originating from Nihonbashi, namely the Tokaido, Nakasendo, Koshu Kaido, Oshu Kaido, and Nikko Kaido. During the Edo period, these routes were meticulously developed under the direction of the shogunate, with checkpoints to regulate travelers, mile markers to indicate distance, inns for resting travelers, and pine trees planted along the way. The major arterial roads emanating from Nihonbashi today still trace the routes of these five historical highways.

第三章

五街道 ごかいどう

日本橋を起点にのびる5つの街道、すなわち東海道、中山道、甲州街道、奥州街道、日光街道のこと。江戸時代、幕府の主導で、通行人を取り締まる関所、距離を示す一里塚、旅人が休むための宿場、さらには街道沿いに松を植えるなどして道が整備された。現在でも日本橋からのびる主要な幹線道路は、この江戸時代の五街道がもとになっている。

Chapter 5

hosoban

The smallest among commonly circulated ukiyo-e print formats, such as *oban* and *chuban*. Measuring approximately 33 cm × 15 cm, the size is equivalent to one-third—sometimes one quarter, depending on the paper—of a full sheet of small-size *hosho* paper, a type of paper made from *kozo*, the bark of the paper mulberry tree. Often used for actor prints during short theater runs, *hosoban* prints were considered the most affordable format and were often printed on thin, low-quality paper.

第五章

細判 ほそばん

大判、中判といった一般的に多く流通した浮世絵版画の判型の中では、画面が最も小さいもの。小奉書（楮製）全紙判の三つ切（紙の種類によっては四つ切）のサイズで、およそ33cm×15cmの大きさ。芝居の上演されている短期間に売り時が限られる役者絵に多く、最も安価な商品として制作されたと考えられ、しばしば薄く質の良くない紙のことがある。

joruri

A form of narrative art accompanied by the *shamisen*, in which the *tayu* (narrator) recites the text. *Joruri* is said to be narrated rather than sung due to the inclusion of character dialogue, emotions, and plot details. As a form of music for kabuki, it is also performed as an accompaniment to *shosagoto* (kabuki dance). *Joruri* is divided into schools, such as *Gidayu-bushi*, according to narrative style, with each tradition being preserved and passed down to the present day.

浄瑠璃 じょうるり

三味線を伴奏楽器として、太夫が詞章を語るもの。「歌う」ではなく「語る」というのは、詞章が登場人物のセリフや気持ち、筋書きといった内容を含むからである。歌舞伎音楽としては、所作事（舞踊）の伴奏として演じられる。その語り口により、義太夫節など「○○節」と呼ばれる流派に分かれ、現在に至るまでその芸が継承されている。

Ichikawa Danjuro

A title for kabuki actors, passed down from the first generation (1660-1704) to the current thirteenth generation (1977-). The name is synonymous with the powerful, acrobatic *aragoto* (rough style) method of kabuki performance it created. Overwhelming popularity for the style, particularly in Edo, led to the production of numerous ukiyo-e works depicting plays featuring Ichikawa Danjuro. The seventh-generation actor in the lineage established the *Kabuki Juhachiban* (Eighteen Best Kabuki Plays) repertoire, from which several works are still frequently performed today.

市川團十郎
いちかわだんじゅうろう

歌舞伎役者の名跡で、初代（1660–1704）から現代の十三代目（1977–）まで、その芸が引き継がれている。力強いアクロバティックな荒事と呼ばれる歌舞伎の演技を創始継承した役者の名として知られており、特に江戸での圧倒的な人気から、出演した芝居は浮世絵に多く題材とされている。七代目は、市川家の荒事芸を歌舞伎十八番として制定し、そのうちいくつかの演目は、現代でもしばしば上演されている。

__Chapter 6__

oiran

The highest-ranking courtesans of the Yoshiwara pleasure quarters. *Oiran* would entertain wealthy and educated patrons, adhering strictly to the unique customs and regulations of Yoshiwara, which included simulated wedding ceremonies and pseudo-marriages prohibiting infidelity even on the part of the patron. More than simply objects of beauty, Yoshiwara's opulently dressed *oiran* were skilled in various arts and required to be highly cultured. Although ukiyo-e prints were an art form enjoyed by the masses, these high-ranking courtesans, figures of adoration and admiration, were depicted across many prints.

第六章

花魁 おいらん

吉原遊廓で特に位の高い遊女を呼ぶ言葉。このような遊女は、裕福で教養のある人物を馴染み客として迎えるが、秩序と独特の習慣を重んじる吉原では、仮の祝言を挙げて擬似夫婦となり、客といえども浮気は許されなかった。豪華な衣装を身につけた花魁は、美しいばかりでなく諸芸に通じ、教養を磨くことが求められた。庶民中心に享受された浮世絵版画だが、花魁は憧れの姿でもあり、このような高位の遊女を描くことが多かった。

Ukiyo-e Artists | 浮世絵師

Torii school

Founded by Torii Kiyonobu (1664-1729), the Torii school has produced theater signboards for over 300 years, continuing the tradition up to the late ninth-generation head, Kiyomitsu IX (1938-2021). The school greatly contributed to the popularization of ukiyo-e prints, fueled by widespread public enthusiasm for kabuki theater.

鳥居派 とりいは

鳥居清信(きよのぶ)(1664-1729)を初代とする鳥居派は、現代の九代目清光(きよみつ)(1938-2021)に至るまで、300年以上にわたり代々芝居小屋の絵看板制作を家業とした。浮世絵版画では、大衆の歌舞伎人気に支えられ、その普及に最も貢献した流派といえる。

Katsukawa Shunsho

(1743-92)

Renowned for his actor and sumo wrestler prints, Katsukawa Shunsho was the first artist to capture the true likeness of his subjects, earning him great popularity. His significant contribution to the development of ukiyo-e established realistic portrayal as a new standard for commercially successful actor prints. A phenomenal talent, he also left behind exceptional hand-painted *bijinga*.

勝川春章

かつかわしゅんしょう
(1743-92)

役者絵や相撲絵の錦絵で、人物の容貌を似顔で描くことを始めて人気を得た絵師。その功績は大きく、春章以降、役者絵は似顔で描くことが商品として成功するための条件となった。その卓越した画才で、優れた肉筆美人画を残したことでも知られている。

Torii Kiyonaga
(1752-1815)

Within the *bijinga* genre, Torii Kiyonaga was celebrated for his tall, graceful beauties set against realistic Edo backdrops. A member of the Torii school, he also gained attention for introducing a new style of actor prints that portrayed kabuki actors onstage with accompanying *joruri* musicians and chanters.

Kitagawa Utamaro
(d. 1806)

Making his ukiyo-e debut under the guidance of publisher Tsutaya Juzaburo, Kitagawa Utamaro excelled in *bijinga*. Notably, he introduced the *ookubi-e* format, capturing subjects' faces prominently. His ability to convey the emotions of women through subtle gestures and postures earned him high acclaim, showcasing his rich expressive talent.

鳥居清長
とりいきよなが
(1752-1815)

美人画では、江戸の現実的な風景を背景に長身で伸びやかなスタイルの美人群像を描いた作品で知られている。鳥居派の絵師でもあるが、役者絵では歌舞伎舞台での所作を出語りとともに描く新しいスタイルの役者絵を出したことでも注目される。

喜多川歌麿
きたがわうたまろ
(?-1806)

版元・蔦屋重三郎(つたやじゅうざぶろう)のプロデュースにより錦絵界にデビューした歌麿は、美人画に優れた作品を多く残した。とりわけ顔を大きく捉えて描く大首絵を美人画に導入し、わずかな仕草や姿勢で、女性の心情まで察せられるような豊かな表現力が評価されている。

Katsushika Hokusai
(1760-1849)

Originally a pupil of Katsukawa Shunsho, Katsushika Hokusai's career spanned some 70 years, producing works across numerous genres. His famous series *Thirty-six Views of Mount Fuji* led to his departure from ukiyo-e prints in 1835 to focus on hand paintings and drawing manuals.

Kitao Masanobu
(1761-1816)

The artistic pseudonym of popular fiction writer Santo Kyoden, Kitao Masanobu was known for his *bijinga*, actor prints, and *kibyoshi* (yellow-covered picture book) illustrations. When Tsutaya Juzaburo ventured into woodblock print publication, Masanobu took on the commemorative *The Handwriting of Modern Beauties in Yoshiwara* series.

葛飾北斎
かつしかほくさい
(1760-1849)

当初は勝川春章の弟子で、作画期は約70年にわたる。多様なジャンルに優れた作品を残しているが、代表作「冨嶽三十六景」シリーズの大ヒット後まもなくの天保6年（1835）には錦絵界を離れ、肉筆画や絵手本類の制作に集中している。

北尾政演
きたおまさのぶ
(1761-1816)

戯作者として活躍した山東京伝の浮世絵師としての画号。黄表紙の挿絵を中心に、美人画や役者絵などを手がけた。蔦屋重三郎が錦絵出版に乗り出した時には、記念碑的作品『吉原傾城新美人合自筆鏡』の遊女絵を手がけている。

Toshusai Sharaku

Published with high expectations by Tsutaya Juzaburo, Toshusai Sharaku's debut was a series of twenty-eight richly illustrated *ookubi-e* portraits of kabuki actors. However, lack of popular appeal at the time led to Sharaku's swift disappearance from the ukiyo-e scene within a year. It was not until their discovery by modern Western collectors of ukiyo-e that Sharaku's talent found critical appreciation. Though his true identity is unclear, one prominent theory suggests that Sharaku was actually the noh theater actor Saito Jurobe (1763-1820) of the Tokushima Domain.

東洲斎写楽

とうしゅうさいしゃらく

(生没年不詳)

デビュー作は豪華な役者大首絵の28図で、版元・蔦屋重三郎が期待した絵師だったと思われる。当時は不人気ゆえに、1年もしないうちに錦絵界から消えてしまったが、写楽を最初に評価したのは、近代西洋の浮世絵コレクターたちだった。徳島藩お抱えの能役者斎藤十郎兵衛(1763-1820)その人であったという説が有力である。

Utagawa Toyokuni III

(*Utagawa Kunisada*) (1786-1864)

A student of Utagawa Toyokuni I (1769-1825), Kunisada showed artistic talent from an early age. He produced more than 10,000 works over his lifetime, including actor prints, *bijinga*, book illustrations, and *Genji-e* (Tale of Genji prints). First going by the name Kunisada, after his master's death he led the Utagawa school as Toyokuni III.

三代歌川豊国(歌川国貞)

さんだいうたがわとよくに

(うたがわくにさだ)

(1786-1864)

初代歌川豊国(1769-1825)の弟子にあたる。少年時代から画才に長けていたと伝えられ、役者絵、美人画、版本の挿絵、源氏絵等、膨大な作品数は1万点を超えるとされる。初め国貞、師の豊国が没した後は豊国を襲名、歌川派を率いる存在となった。

Keisai Eisen
(1790-1848)

Active from the early to mid-nineteenth century, following the death of Kitagawa Utamaro, Keisai Eisen's oeuvre includes numerous outstanding *bijinga* works rich with decadence and sensuality. Although later replaced by Utagawa Hiroshige for unknown reasons, Eisen was the artist initially assigned to *The Sixty-nine Stations of the Kiso Kaido* series, indicating his skill in landscapes as well.

Utagawa Kuniyasu
(1794-1832)

A prized student of Utagawa Toyokuni I, Kuniyasu was known for his actor prints and depictions of daily life. His works often feature scenes busy with people, skillfully portraying the distinct expressions of each individual within the crowd.

溪斎英泉
けいさいえいせん
(1790-1848)

歌麿亡き後の文化末年頃から弘化期（1818－48）に主に美人画で活躍。退廃的で濃厚な色香を漂わす美人画に代表作が多くある。何らかの理由により途中で歌川広重と交代した壮大な「木曽街道六拾九次（きそかいどうろくじゅうきゅうつぎ）」シリーズを最初に任されていることから、風景画においても期待された絵師であったことがわかる。

歌川国安
うたがわくにやす
(1794-1832)

初代歌川豊国の高弟の一人で、役者絵や生活風俗を描いた作品などが知られている。大勢の人物を描き込み、それぞれの表情を描き分けた群衆描写も得意としていた。

Utagawa Hiroshige
(1797-1858)

Although born into a family of Edo firefighters, whose duty it was to protect the city from the threat of fire, Hiroshige quickly became a student of artist Utagawa Toyohiro (d. 1829). Starting with the popular and commercial success of his *The Fifty-three Stations of the Tokaido* series, he went on to produce countless exceptional landscapes, helping to establish the landscape print genre alongside Katsushika Hokusai.

Utagawa Kuniyoshi
(1797-1861)

Celebrated for his dynamic series *One Hundred and Eight Heroes of the Popular Water Margin*, Utagawa Kuniyoshi earned the moniker "master of warrior prints." Nevertheless, his versatility is evident from the various landscapes he produced using Western perspective and shading techniques, as well as humorous *giga* (satirical prints) and *bijinga.*

歌川広重
うたがわひろしげ
(1797-1858)

定火消同心（江戸の防火、警備を行う役割）の家に生まれ跡を継いだが、ほどなく歌川豊広（?-1829）の弟子となった。「東海道五拾三次之内」シリーズのヒットをきっかけに、優れた風景画を多く制作し、葛飾北斎とともに浮世絵における風景画というジャンルの確立に貢献した。

歌川国芳
うたがわくによし
(1797-1861)

躍動感あふれる「通俗水滸伝豪傑百八人之一人」シリーズで成功をおさめ、「武者絵の国芳」と評された。一方で、西洋の遠近法や陰影描写を取り込んだ風景画や、ユーモラスな戯画、生活風俗を描く美人画など、幅広い分野に親しみやすい優れた画才を発揮した。

Tsukioka Yoshitoshi
(1839-92)

One of the leading ukiyo-e artists of the Meiji period, Tsukioka Yoshitoshi was a student of Utagawa Kuniyoshi. A sense of realism, influenced by Western art, lends a unique character to his warrior prints, historical prints, and *bijinga*.

月岡芳年
つきおかよしとし
(1839-92)

明治期を代表する浮世絵師の一人で、歌川国芳の門人。西洋画の影響による実在感のある人物描写で、武者絵、歴史画、美人画に独特の個性を発揮した。

Appendix

Museums to Visit

付録

訪ねてみたい美術館

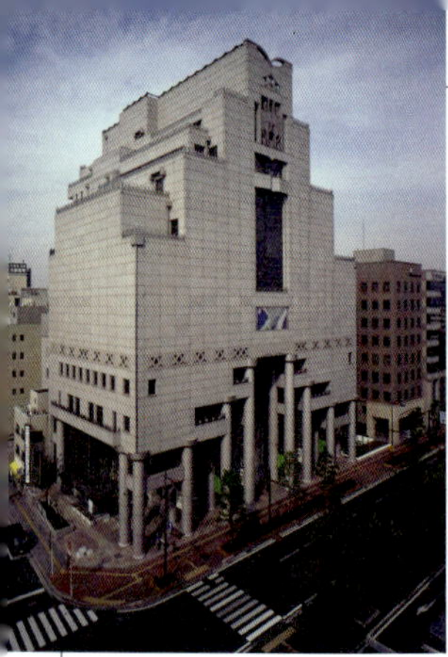

Chiba City Museum of Art

Boasting one of the most prestigious ukiyo-e collections in Japan, the Chiba City Museum of Art's collection strategy emphasizes three main areas: Japanese paintings and prints from the early modern to modern periods; contemporary art since 1945; and works related to Boso, with a focus on Chiba City, where the museum is located. Designed using the traditional Japanese *sayado* (sheath hall) method, it encloses one of the city's pre-WWII cultural heritage sites, the former Chiba Branch of the Kawasaki Bank originally built in 1927, within the new structure. Following a renewal in 2020, the permanent exhibition room now features highlights from the collection, displaying ukiyo-e prints on monthly rotation.

千葉市美術館

国内でも屈指の浮世絵コレクションを誇る美術館。館蔵品の収集方針としては「近世から近代の日本絵画と版画」、「1945年以降の現代美術」、そして館が立地する「千葉市を中心とした房総ゆかりの作品」の3つを柱としている。美術館建築も特徴的で、1927年築の旧川崎銀行千葉支店を包み込むように新しい建物で覆い、日本古来の伝統工法の鞘堂(さやどう)方式が用いられている。2020年のリニューアルによって新設された、コレクションのハイライトを紹介する常設展示室では浮世絵が月ごとに展示替えされている。

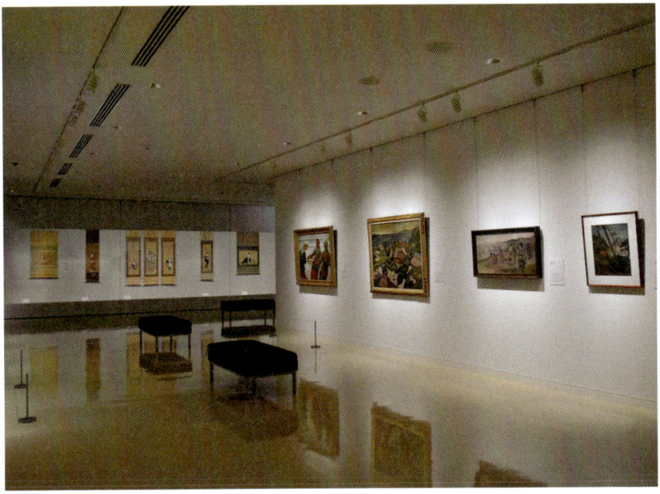

Address: 3-10-8 Chuo, Chuo-ku, Chiba City, Chiba Prefecture
Telephone: 043-221-2311
Hours: 10:00-18:00 (Fridays and Saturdays 10:00-20:00)
Closed: First Monday of each month (or the following day if a national holiday), year-end and New Year's holidays (12/29-1/3), and during maintenance
Admission (Permanent Exhibition): General, 300 yen; university students, 220 yen; free of charge for elementary, middle, and high school students, Chiba Prefecture residents aged 65 and over, individuals with a disability certificate and their caregivers, and special exhibition ticket holders
**Admission fees for special exhibitions vary by exhibition. Please check the website for details.*
URL: https://www.ccma-net.jp/

住所：千葉県千葉市中央区中央3-10-8
電話：043-221-2311　営業時間：10：00～18：00（金・土曜日は20：00まで）
休館日：毎月第1月曜日（祝日の場合は翌日）、
年末年始（12月29日～1月3日）、メンテナンス日
観覧料（常設展示室）：一般300円、大学生220円、小・中学生、高校生、
千葉県内在住の65歳以上の方、障害者手帳をお持ちの方とその介護者、
企画展観覧の方は無料
※企画展示室の観覧料は展覧会ごとに異なるので、詳細はホームページで確認のこと
URL：https://www.ccma-net.jp/

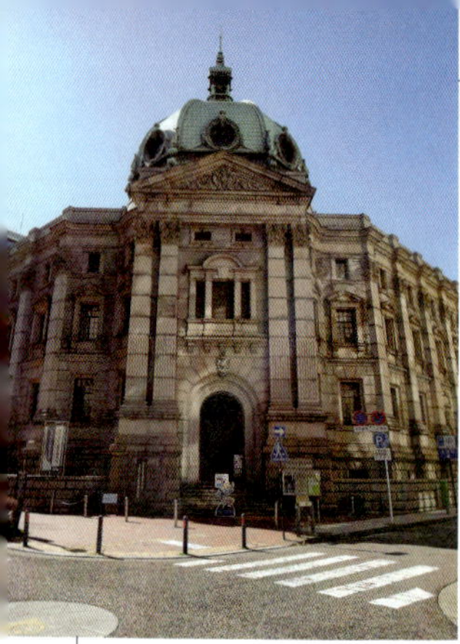

Kanagawa Prefectural Museum of Cultural History

Kanagawa Prefectural Museum of Cultural History is the only museum providing a comprehensive overview of Kanagawa Prefecture's culture and history. Among its permanent exhibition rooms, the floors for "The Highways and Popular Culture of Early Modern Times" and "Modernization and the Opening of Yokohama's Port" feature numerous ukiyo-e collections. Within the permanent exhibition rooms, topic-specific exhibitions also showcase ukiyo-e prints across rich and diverse themes. The museum consists of two parts: a historic neo-baroque building from 1904, the original façade of which has been carefully preserved, as well as a newly added extension, and is now designated as a national important cultural property.

神奈川県立歴史博物館

「かながわの文化と歴史」を総合的に扱う唯一の博物館。常設展示室の「近世の街道と庶民文化」と「横浜開港と近代化」のフロアで、浮世絵コレクションの数々が展示されている。また、常設展室内のトピック展示として、変化に富んだテーマで浮世絵を紹介している。博物館の建物は、1904年に建てられたネオ・バロック様式の旧館と増築された新館部分から成り立ち、旧館部分の外観は建築当初の姿をそのまま残し、国の重要文化財の指定を受けている。

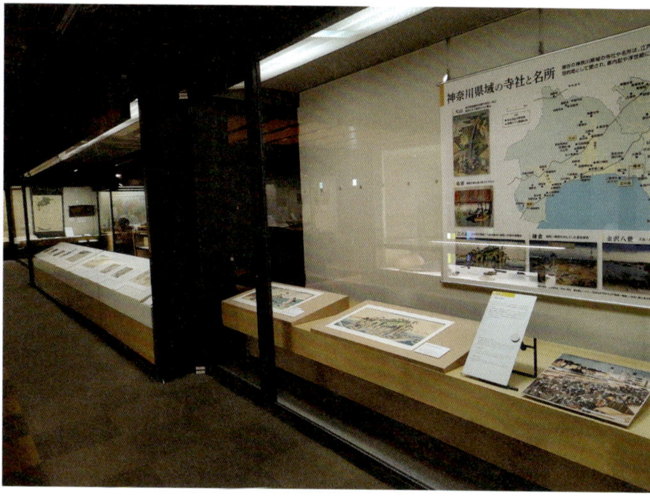

Address: 5-60 Minami-Nakadori, Naka-ku, Yokohama City, Kanagawa Prefecture Telephone: 045-201-0926 Hours: 9:30-17:00
Closed: Mondays (open on national holidays), year-end and New Year's holidays (12/28–1/4), and during exhibit changes and other temporary closures
Admission (Permanent Exhibition): Adults aged 20 and over, 300 yen; students and visitors under 20, 200 yen; high school students and those aged 65 and over, 100 yen; free of charge for junior high school students and under, and individuals with a disability certificate
**Special exhibitions require a separate fee. Please check the website for details.*
URL: https://ch.kanagawa-museum.jp/

住所：神奈川県横浜市中区南仲通5-60
電話：045-201-0926　営業時間：9：30～17：00
休館日：月曜日（祝日の場合は開館）、年末年始（12月28日～1月4日）、
資料整理休館日、その他臨時休館日
観覧料（常設展）：20歳以上の方300円、学生の方・20歳未満の方200円、
高校生の方・65歳以上の方100円、
中学生以下の方・障害者手帳をお持ちの方は無料
※特別展は別料金になるため、詳細はホームページの開催情報で確認のこと
URL：https://ch.kanagawa-museum.jp/

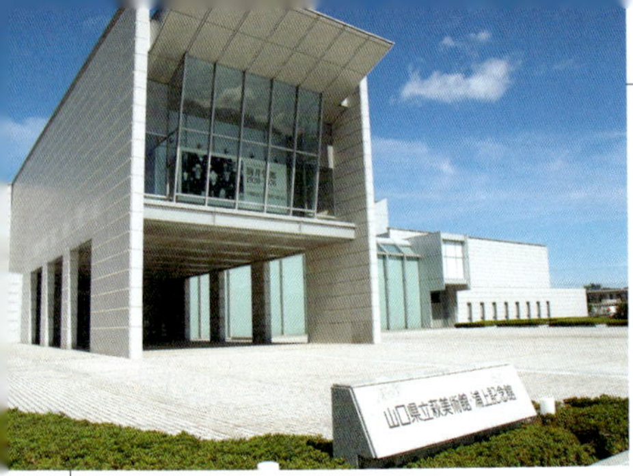

Hagi Uragami Museum

The Hagi Uragami Museum was established following the donation of the Uragami Collection, featuring ukiyo-e and East Asian ceramics collected by businessman Uragami Toshiro (1926-2020) from Hagi City, Yamaguchi Prefecture. The museum boasts a collection of over 5,500 ukiyo-e prints, of which around 30 prints are selected each month and displayed according to different themes. The collection includes outstanding works by renowned artists such as Hokusai, Utamaro, Sharaku, and Hiroshige, providing a comprehensive view of ukiyo-e history and making the museum a valuable center for ukiyo-e research both domestically and overseas.

山口県立萩美術館・浦上記念館

山口県萩市出身の実業家・浦上敏朗氏（1926-2020）が収集した浮世絵、東洋陶磁を中心とした「浦上コレクション」が県に寄贈されたことを契機に設立された美術館。所有する浮世絵は5500点以上の点数を誇り、その中から毎月テーマ別に約30点を選定して展示を行っている。北斎、歌麿、写楽、広重などの主要絵師の優品をはじめ、浮世絵の歴史を通覧できる幅広いコレクションがあり、国内外の浮世絵研究のための貴重な拠点となっている。

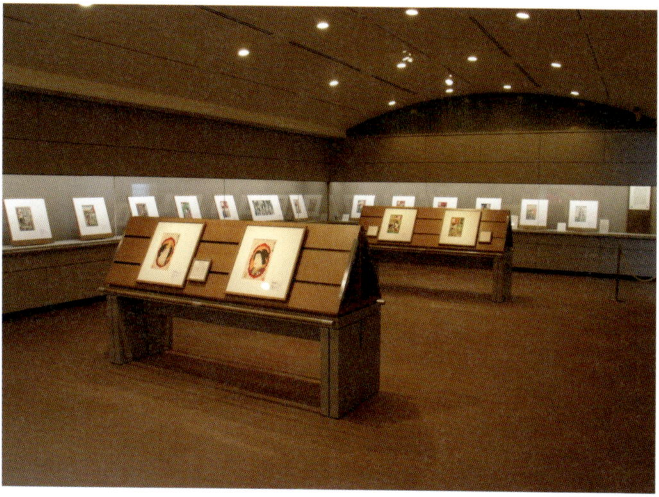

Address: 586-1 Hiyako-machi, Hagi City, Yamaguchi Prefecture
Telephone: 0838-24-2400 Hours: 9:00-17:00
Closed: Mondays (open on national holidays and the first Monday of the month), year-end and New Year's holidays, and during exhibition changes and maintenance
Admission (Permanent Collection): General, 300 yen; students, 200 yen; free of charge for those aged 70 and over, 18 and under, high school and junior high school students, and students of special support schools
**Admission fees for special exhibitions vary by exhibition. Please check the website for details.*
URL: https://hum-web.jp/

住所：山口県萩市平安古町586-1
電話：0838-24-2400 営業時間：9：00～17：00
休館日：月曜日（祝日の場合は開館、第1月曜日は開館）、
年末年始、展示替え、館内整備等臨時休館日
観覧料（コレクション展）：一般300円、学生の方200円、
70歳以上と18歳以下の方、高校生・中学生・特別支援学校に在籍の方は無料
※特別展により観覧料が異なるため、詳細はホームページの開催情報で確認のこと
URL：https://hum-web.jp/

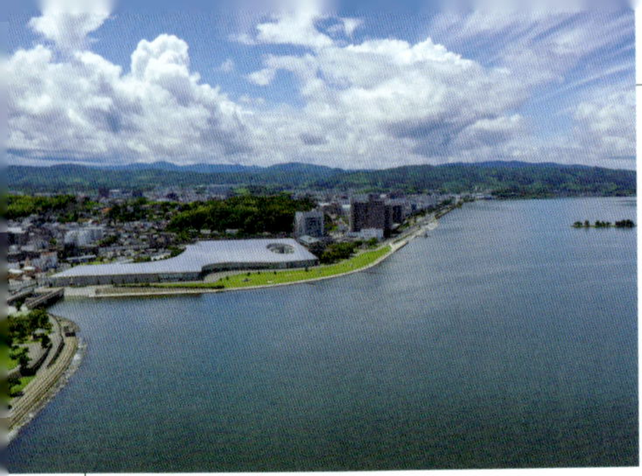

Shimane Art Museum

Situated on the shore of Lake Shinji, the Shimane Art Museum offers breathtaking views over the water and a sunset selected as one of Japan's 100 most beautiful. The museum houses a collection of approximately 3,000 ukiyo-e prints, including an extensive array of masterpieces by globally acclaimed artists Katsushika Hokusai and Utagawa Hiroshige. The core of the collection was donated by businessman Shinjo Jiro (1901-96), from Matsue, and Hokusai researcher Nagata Seiji (1951-2018), from Tsuwano, in addition to further works purchased by Shimane Prefecture. The museum's Hokusai Exhibition Room exists as a dedicated space for the display of approximately 40 woodblock prints and hand-painted works by Hokusai.

島根県立美術館

宍道湖畔に立つ、「日本の夕陽百選」にも選ばれた湖上の景観を観賞できる美術館。約3000点の浮世絵を所蔵し、その中核をなすのが松江市出身の実業家・新庄二郎氏（1901-96）と津和野町出身の北斎研究家・永田生慈氏（1951-2018）によるコレクションで、これに島根県が購入した作品群で構成されている。特に葛飾北斎と歌川広重の代表作が網羅されており、世界に誇る優品がそろう。館内の「北斎展示室」は常時約40点の北斎の木版画と肉筆画が鑑賞できる特別な場所となっている。

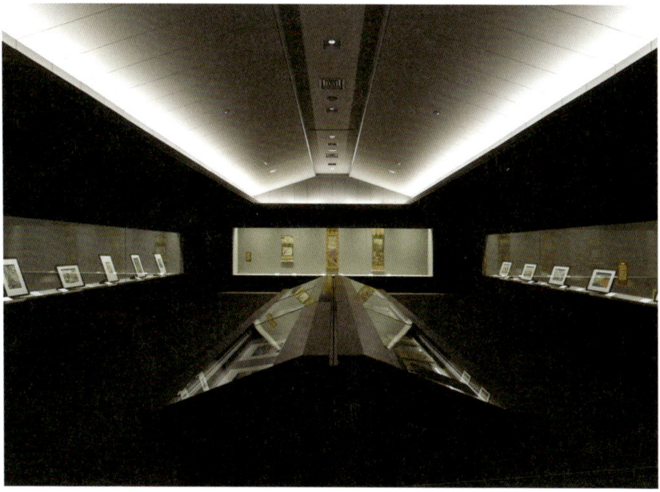

Address: 1-5 Sodeshi-cho, Matsue City, Shimane Prefecture
Telephone: 0852-55-4700
Hours: 10:00-18:30 (October to February); 10:00-30 minutes after sunset (March to September)
Closed: Tuesdays, year-end and New Year's holidays, and other closures according to special exhibition schedules
Admission (Permanent Collection): General, 300 yen; university students, 200 yen; free of charge for high school students and under
**Admission fees for special exhibitions vary by exhibition. Please check the website for details.*
URL: https://www.shimane-art-museum.jp/

住所：島根県松江市袖師町1-5
電話：0852-55-4700
営業時間：【10月〜2月】10：00〜18：30
【3月〜9月】10：00〜日没後30分
休館日：火曜日、年末年始、企画展の開催日程等にあわせて変更する場合がある
観覧料（コレクション展）：一般300円、大学生200円、高校生以下は無料
※企画展は観覧料が異なるため、詳細はホームページの開催情報で確認のこと
URL：https://www.shimane-art-museum.jp/

田辺昌子　たなべ・まさこ
国際浮世絵学会常任理事。東京都生まれ。
学習院大学人文科学研究科博士前期課程修了、
美学美術史専攻。永青文庫学芸員を経て、
元千葉市美術館副館長。
鈴木春信を中心に浮世絵の研究に携わる。
『鳥居清長』展図録で
第1回國華賞展覧会図録賞（共同受賞、2008年）、
『菱川師宣と浮世絵の誕生 房州から江戸へ』で
第30回國華賞受賞（2018年）。
『もっと知りたい喜多川歌麿』（東京美術、2024年）
など著書多数。

編集
竹内清乃

装丁・本文デザイン
金田一亜弥　髙畠なつみ（金田一デザイン）

英訳
Alex G. K. Pulsford

校正
小学館出版クォリティーセンター

Bilingual Guide to Japan
UKIYO-E

浮世絵バイリンガルガイド

2024年10月1日　初版　第1刷発行

著　者　田辺昌子
発行者　斎藤 満

発行所　株式会社小学館
〒101－8001
東京都千代田区一ツ橋2－3－1
編集　03－3230－5563
販売　03－5281－3555

印刷所　大日本印刷株式会社
製本所　株式会社若林製本工場
D T P　株式会社昭和ブライト

編　集　矢野文子(小学館)

造本には十分注意しておりますが、印刷、製本など製造上の不備がございましたら「制作局コールセンター」(フリーダイヤル0120-336-340)にご連絡ください。(電話受付は、土・日・祝休日を除く 9:30～17:30)
本書の無断での複写(コピー)、上演、放送等の二次利用、翻案等は、著作権法上の例外を除き禁じられています。本書の電子データ化などの無断複製は著作権法上の例外を除き禁じられています。代行業者等の第三者による本書の電子的複製も認められておりません。

©2024 Masako Tanabe
Printed in Japan
ISBN 978-4-09-389171-4